Savour
Press

Delectable
dessert,
pastry,
tart
Recipes
in this
Tart
Cookbook

tarts!

TARTS!

DELECTABLE DESSERT, PASTRY, TART RECIPES IN THIS TART COOKBOOK!

By
Savour Press

Published by
Savour Press, a DBA of Wentworth Publishing House

Savour Press

Let's get it started!

Welcome to Savour. We always love food ever since we were kids, and that's because food plays a focal point in our everyday lives. Without it, we feel weak, frail and sick. It is with this thrust that you try your best to discover recipes that could bring your loved ones together in one occasion or during dinner time. One of the foods that are most anticipated in your gatherings is dessert tarts, which can be eaten for brunch, breakfast, dinner and on special occasions. Tarts are easy to prepare if you know the sequence. Though most tart recipes have a long list of instructions, they are not really difficult to follow. This is why we filled up this book with 45 most delicious dessert tart recipes for you to follow, and not meant to drive you crazy. Learn the basics of tart preparation and in the end you will find them stress-relieving. Yes, they help relax your mind, and the finished product will give you fulfillment, seeing other people enjoy your tarts.

About This Book

You love tarts the way you love cakes and other desserts, but the idea of preparing them for your own pleasure and satisfaction of your family and friends may be far from your mind. The reason may be that you have a negative impression on how it is prepared. Yes, it is true that most tart recipes have complicated instructions because you have to prepare the crust by pulsing the ingredients, roll them into dough, press them into the bottom of the tart pan, and freeze them for thirty minutes, and then place a foil on top and pie weights, bake, then remove the foil and pie weights and bake again. Then you have to prepare the caramel, ganache, filling, assemble the topping, sprinkle the glaze, etc. This is just a sample how it is prepared, and there are many ways of preparing them, including the flavors and their taste. *Savour* does not want to put you down; instead we are here to guide you on how to prepare the most delicious dessert tarts that will leave positive feedbacks from your loved ones.

Let's get ready to have a fun time!

Also, by the editors at Savour Press's kitchen

The Chili Cookbook

The Quiche Cookbook

The Cajun and Creole Cookbook

The Grill Cookbook

The Burger Book

The Ultimate Appetizers Cookbook

The West African Cookbook

Korean Seoul Cookbook

The Cast Iron Cookbook

The Holiday Cookbook

The Baking Book

The Crepe Cookbook

CONTENTS

INTRODUCTION

Tarts like other desserts are really pleasing to your taste buds, even if you are not a sweet tooth. The sweet taste and creamy filling of various mixtures (chocolate, cream cheese, caramel, mousse, mocha, curd, swirls, etc.) are comforting. They make your day great, and will complete your meal. You need some equipment to prepare the tarts like a blender or food processor to pulse the crust ingredients into coarse meal, pea-sized crumbles, or into fine powder. You also need rectangular and round tart pans or if you like mini tarts or tartlets, use mini tart pans. When baking the tarts you have to put the tart pans on a baking sheet for possible drippings and some recipes requires you push the dough into the bottom after blind baking as they tend to puff out or prick them beforehand with fork. These are some of the things that you should know when preparing the tarts. But as you keep on reading, your knowledge keeps on increasing.

Enjoy!

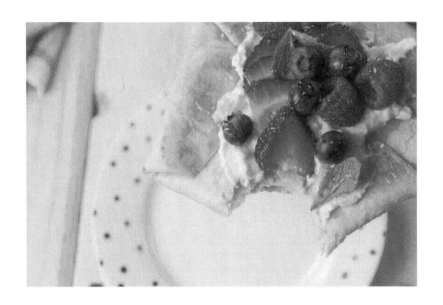

Summer Berry Tortilla Tart

You don't need to be skillful in baking to prepare a cheesy and creamy tortilla tart. Use your oven toaster to brown the folded tortilla and top it with ricotta, berries, honey and mint. The sweet and buttery crust will make you ask for more.

Servings: 2

Ingredients

2 pieces **6" or 8" flour tortillas**

Pat of softened **butter**

Pinch of **white sugar**

1/2 cup **whole milk ricotta cheese**

Assorted berries

Honey

Fresh **mint leaves**

DIRECTIONS:

Preheat the oven at 400 degrees F.

Brush both sides of flour tortillas with butter and sprinkle with sugar. Fold over one inch sections of each tortilla in clockwise direction.

Wet the surface of each section with a droplet of water and fold down the edge, and then fold down the edges in overlapping style.

Press with your thumb the folds, placing the top side down on the baking sheet. Finish the second tortilla with these steps.

Poke holes on the tortillas with fork tines to avoid bubbling. Cook for 5 to 7 minutes in your toaster oven until golden.

Slowly flip the other side and cook for 5 minutes until golden. Remove from toaster oven and let cool.

Evenly spread ricotta on the folded side of the tart. Spread on top with assorted berries and drizzle with honey.

Garnish tart with fresh mint.

Serve!

Nutritional Information: 731 calorie; 7.7 g fat (4.5 g saturated fat); 25 mg cholesterol; 91 mg sodium; 158.3 g carbohydrate; 1.9 g dietary fiber; 129.2 g total sugars; 8.7 g protein.

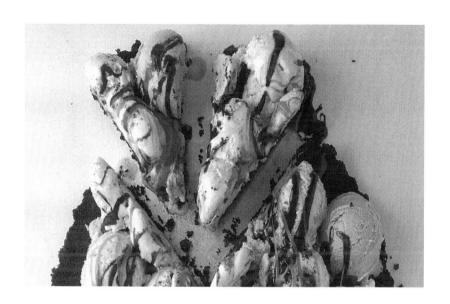

OREOGASM ICE CREAM TART

Oreos are great for preparing an ice cream tart if you know nothing about baking. Use a food processor to pulse the cookies until it forms fine crumbs and press into a springform pan. Freeze to firm up and spread with ice cream. Top with melted cookies 'n crème bars and drizzle with chocolate sauce.

Servings: 6

Ingredients

30 **Oreo cookies**

1 stick **melted butter**

12 scoops **cookies 'n cream ice cream**

2 melted **Hershey's Cookies 'n Creme bars**

Chocolate sauce

Directions

Prepare the ingredients by scraping the frosting of Oreo cookies and pulse in your food processor with metal blade until they turn into fine crumbs.

Add the melted butter to the processor and pulse until incorporated.

Place the Oreo crust in a nine-inch springform pan, pressing lightly until firmly adhere.

Freeze for half an hour until firm. Remove the springform pan and place over tart a scoop of ice cream.

Drizzle on top with cookies 'n crème bars and chocolate sauce. Slice into six.

Note: Freeze for another ten minutes if the ice cream is soft to slice.

Enjoy!

Nutritional Information: 996 calorie; 58 g fat (29.7 g saturated fat); 142 mg cholesterol; 689 mg sodium; 108.5 g carbohydrate; 3.8 g dietary fiber; 79.7 g total sugars; 14.2 g protein.

RHUBARB TART

The long list of ingredients and instructions is worth the effort with this adorable tart. The creamy shortbread crust is filled with sweet frangipane filling which is composed of almond meal, dark rum, butter, zest, egg, butter, vanilla and almond. The tart slices are topped with lattice patterned rhubarb.

Servings: 8

Ingredients

For the shortbread crust:

1 1/4 cups **all-purpose flour**

1/4 teaspoon **kosher salt**

2/3 cup **powdered sugar**

1 stick (1/2 cup cold) **unsalted butter**, cut into cubes

1/2 teaspoon **vanilla bean paste**

1 tablespoon **heavy cream**

1 **egg yolk**

For the frangipane filling:

1 tablespoon **unsalted butter**

1/3 cup **granulated sugar**

3/4 cups **almond meal**

1 tablespoon **dark rum**

1 large **egg**

1/2 teaspoon **lemon zest**

1/2 teaspoon **vanilla bean paste**

1/8 teaspoon **kosher salt**

1/4 teaspoon **almond extract**

For the rhubarb lattice topping:

8 to 10 stalks fresh **rhubarb**

1/2 cup **granulated sugar**

1 cup **water**

Directions

Prepare the shortbread crust:

In a food processor, pulse together the flour, salt and powdered sugar until combined, and then add the butter.

Pulse until the mixture looks like coarse meal. Stir in a small bowl the egg, vanilla and cream and pour into the food processor while still processing until the dough forms into a ball.

Remove the dough from food processor, wrap in plastic wrap and refrigerate for thirty minutes.

Preheat the oven at 375 degrees Fahrenheit. Roll into 3/16" thick and transfer to a tart pan. Trim excess dough.

Line aluminum foil and pie weights made of ceramic. Bake for fifteen minutes until golden.

Prepare the frangipane filling:

Cook the butter in a small saucepan on medium heat until it turns nutty-brown, set aside and slightly cool.

Stir in a bowl the almond meal, egg, sugar, vanilla, rum, salt, zest and almond extract until well combined.

Fold in the browned butter and transfer to the half-baked tart shell.

Bake for thirty minutes until set and golden brown. Let cool and cover with rhubarb lattice.

Prepare the rhubarb lattice topping:

With a mandolin slicer, slice the rhubarb lengthwise with a thickness of 1/16 inch.

Fill a pot with water and sugar; bring to a boil and add four to five slices of rhubarb. Simmer on low until softened. Drain rhubarb on paper towels. Boil the rhubarb in batches until nothing left, saving the remaining syrup.

On a sheet of parchment paper, line up the rhubarb slices side-by-side. Fold the alternating slices facing up and then some slices in vertical arrangement on top to form a lattice design.

Repeat the process until the lattice becomes bigger to cover the surface of the tart.

Flip the parchment paper onto the surface of the cooled tart. Remove the parchment by peeling away and trim off the overhang.

Glaze the lattice with reserved poaching liquid.

Serve!

Nutritional Information: 393 calorie; 20 g fat (9 g saturated fat); 81 mg cholesterol; 122 mg sodium; 28 mg potassium; 48 g carbohydrate; 1 g dietary fiber; 31 g total sugars; 5 g protein.

Caprese Tart with Roasted Tomatoes

This crowd pleaser tart is a joy to your taste buds. The puff pastry is alternately topped with caramelized roasted tomatoes and buffalo mozzarella slices. The edges are brushed with beaten eggs and topped with basil leaves and then baked for a few minutes. This is great for your quick dinner or you can make this ahead of time.

Servings: 6

Ingredients

For the roasted tomatoes:

2 tablespoons **olive oil**

10 **tomatoes** sliced into 1 cm slices

Dash **black pepper**

Pinch **sea salt flakes**

For the tart:

1 roll defrosted **ready-made puff pastry**

1 cup **buffalo mozzarella** or **fior di latte** sliced into 1/2 centimeter slices

1 beaten **egg**

Handful **fresh basil leaves**

Directions

Preheat the oven at 392 degrees F.

On a nonstick baking tray, place the tomato slices and drizzle with olive oil.

Sprinkle tomatoes with salt and pepper and roast for 20 minutes until the edges are caramelized. Remove the tomatoes and slightly cool.

Decrease oven temperature to 356 degrees F.

Prepare the tart by rolling the pastry on a work surface into thin layer.

Place on a baking sheet lined with baking paper. Create a border by scoring the edges, but not cutting through the pastry.

Alternately, place on top of the pastry the caramelized tomatoes and mozzarella. Brush the edges with beaten egg and drizzle with olive oil. Sprinkle on top with salt and pepper.

Bake for 15 to 20 minutes until golden-crisp. Remove tart from oven and garnish with fresh basil leaves.

Serve!

Nutritional Information: 144 calorie; 9.6 g fat (2.2 g saturated fat; 30 mg cholesterol; 118 mg sodium; 11.7 g carbohydrate; 2.6 g dietary fiber; 5.5 g total sugars; 4.6 g protein.

APPLE WALNUT TART WITH MAPLE CUSTARD

You will awe in wonder how the rose designed apple slices is created. It is not difficult to do. First, you have to prepare the walnut crust by mixing the ingredients and bake them. Spread with maple custard on top of crust, and assemble the warmed apple slices into a rose by arranging them in a concentric pattern.

Servings: 10

Ingredients

For the Walnut Crust:

2 1/2 cups **walnut pieces**

2 tablespoons **granulated sugar**

4 tablespoons melted **unsalted butter**

1/4 teaspoon **kosher salt**

1 **egg white**

For the Custard:

1 1/2 cups **1% milk**

1/2 cup **pure maple syrup**

6 **egg yolks**

1/2 teaspoon **kosher salt**

1/4 cup **cornstarch**

1 teaspoon **vanilla extract**

To assemble:

2 **Macoun apples**

Juice of a lemon

1/4 cup warmed **apricot jam**

Directions

For the Walnut Crust:

Preheat the oven at 400 degrees Fahrenheit.

Pulse in a food processor the walnuts until finely chopped until the size resembles breadcrumbs.

Transfer to a large bowl and toss with the remaining ingredients with a fork.

Evenly press onto the bottom and up to the sides of a 9" tart pan with a detachable bottom. Bake for fifteen minutes.

For the Custard:

Heat the milk in a small saucepan on medium heat until the edges form small bubbles.

Whisk in a medium-sized bowl the egg yolks with the cornstarch, maple syrup and salt.

Gently pour the warm milk into the egg mixture, while whisking to warm through.

Return the mixture to the saucepan. Cook and stir on low heat until bubbly and thick.

Add the vanilla and pour into a heat proof container. Cover the container with plastic wrap. Refrigerate for two hours.

Assemble the Tart:

Prepare the apples by cutting into quarters, core and thinly slice. Soak in lemon until ready to use, set aside.

Evenly spread the maple custard in the walnut crust.

Microwave the apples slices, until pliable and roll each into a spiral and let it stand vertically in the custard.

Arrange the slices in a concentric design (or circles sharing the same center), around the first apple slice to create a rose pattern.

Reheat the apricot jam and stir in lemon juice. Use this to glaze the apples to prevent discoloration.

Enjoy!

Nutritional Information: 383 calorie; 26 g fat (5.1 g saturated fat); 140 mg cholesterol; 204 mg cholesterol; 31.4 g carbohydrate; 31.4 g carbohydrate; 3.3 g dietary fiber; 21 g total sugars; 10.9 g protein.

REESE'S CHOCOLATE PEANUT BUTTER TART

This no bake tart is effortless, yet it is loaded with gooey texture and creaminess like no other. The Oreo-butter crust is filled with peanut butter ganache and chilled before spreading the chocolate chip ganache on top and garnished with mini Reese's before chilling to firm up.

Servings: 10 to 12 slices

Ingredients

1 1/2 cups **Oreo crumbs**

4 tablespoons melted **butter**

6 ounces **peanut butter chips**

1 cup **heavy whipping cream**, divided

6 ounces **chocolate chips**

12 to 15 quartered **mini Reese's**

Directions

Combine butter with cookie crumbs until well blended. Press evenly into the bottom and up to the sides of an oiled 9" tart pan with detachable bottom. Set aside.

Place the peanut butter chips in a heat proof bowl together with ½ cup of heavy whipping enough to cover the chips. Microwave for 1 to 2 minutes until the cream starts to boil. Remove bowl from microwave; whisk until smooth.

Evenly spread the peanut butter ganache into the crust. Chill for fifteen minutes until firm.

Meanwhile, place the chocolate chips into a heat proof bowl and combine with the remaining ½ cup heavy whipping cream enough to cover the chips.

Microwave for 1 to 2 minutes until it starts to boil. Remove bowl from microwave; whisk until smooth.

Evenly spread the chocolate ganache on top of the peanut butter ganache.

Arrange on top with mini Reese's. Chill for 1 hour until firm.

Serve!

Nutritional Information: 666 calorie; 41.1 g fat (20.6 g saturated fat); 37 mg cholesterol; 335 mg sodium; 67.9 g carbohydrate; 3.1 g dietary fiber; 55.4 g total sugars; 8.7 g protein.

Glazed Berry Breakfast Tarts

These tarts are excellent partners for your black coffee or tea. Each tart is filled with a spoonful of raspberry or strawberry jam and drizzled with glaze for extra sweet. For variation, you can use other fruit preserves, marmalade or jelly as filling.

Servings: 12

Ingredients

1/4 cup **granulated sugar**

3 cups **all-purpose flour**

1/2 teaspoon **salt**

3/4 teaspoon **baking soda**

4 teaspoons **baking powder**

10 tablespoons **butter**, cut up and cold

3/4 cup **confectioners' sugar**

3/4 cup plus 2 tablespoons **buttermilk**

3/4 cup **raspberry or strawberry jam**

1 tablespoon plus 1 teaspoon **milk**

1/2 teaspoon **vanilla extract**

Optional:

Red food coloring

Coarse **sugar**

Directions

Preheat the oven at 425 degrees F.

Put in a food processor the flour, baking powder, granulated sugar, salt and baking soda. Pulse and add the butter; pulse again until it looks like coarse crumbs.

Place the mixture in a large bowl. Add the butter and stir until the dough is easy to handle.

Place the dough on a surface dusted lightly with flour and divide into half. Roll the dough to form into a 15x10-inch rectangle. Cut the rectangle into six 5" squares.

Spread each square with one tablespoon of jam and wet the edges with a little water. Fold the pastry on top of filling and seal the edges with a fork and prick to form a design.

Place the tarts on a large baking sheet. Do the same steps for the rest of the rectangle dough and raspberry or strawberry jam.

Bake for ten to twelve minutes until golden. Let cool before drizzling the glaze.

Combine in a medium bowl the milk, vanilla, confectioner's sugar and optional food coloring.

Drizzle with glaze and sprinkle with optional coarse sugar.

Serve!

Nutritional Information: 322 calorie; 10 g fat (6.2 g saturated fat); 26 mg cholesterol; 248 mg sodium; 55 g carbohydrate; 0.9 g dietary fiber; 11.7 g total sugars; 3.4 g protein.

Raspberry & Vanilla Bean Cream Tarts

Delight your sweet tooth with these creamy tarts nestled on a shortbread crust and filled with vanilla cream filling. Make the crust before preparing the cream and everything will turn out well. You can opt to use 1 large tart pan or 6 mini tart pans.

Servings: 6 small tarts or 1 large tart

Ingredients

For the shortbread crust:

1/3 cup **sugar**

1 1/4 cup **flour**

Pinch of **salt**

1/2 cup of **butter**

1 **egg yolk**

For the Vanilla Bean Pastry Cream:

4 **egg yolks**

2 tablespoons **cornstarch**

1/3 cup **sugar**

1/2 **vanilla bean**

1 1/3 cups **whole milk**

1/4 to 1/2 teaspoon **vanilla**

For the topping:

Raspberries

Icing sugar

Equipment: 6 inch mini 3 tart pans or 1 large tart pan

Directions

Making the crust:

Preheat the oven at 400 degrees F.

Place in a food processor the flour, salt and sugar and process for ten seconds.

Cut the butter into chunks and add to the mixture; process until the mixture is similar to coarse crumbs.

Add the egg yolk to the mixture, process once more until well combined.

If preparing tartlets or mini tarts, separate the mixture into six three-inch tart pans and then press into the molds with the center lower than the sides. Bake for twelve to fifteen minutes; prick several times with a fork as the dough expands, making sure not to overcook it.

For one large tart, all you have to do is to press the mixture into a ten-inch tart pan with the center lower than the sides.

Bake for fifteen to eighteen minutes. Prick the tart and keep an eye while baking.

For the vanilla cream:

With a hand mixer, beat in a large bowl the cornstarch, sugar and egg yolks until thickened and the color turns pale yellow.

Split the vanilla bean down the center to expose the seed and combine in a small saucepan with milk; let simmer. Ladle the vanilla bean.

Fold half of the milk mixture in egg mixture, stirring often to combine well and return to the remaining of the milk mixture in the saucepan.

Cook and whisk often, until bubbly and thickened to prevent the custard from burning its bottom.

Remove saucepan from heat and add the vanilla. Cover with parchment paper to avoid skin formation; let cool until ready to use.

Assemble Tart:

Add ¼ cup of custard to individual shell when both custard and shells have cooled.

Garnish with fresh raspberries and dust with icing sugar.

Serve!

Nutritional Information: 342 calorie; 21.2 g fat (12.1 g saturated fat); 221 mg cholesterol; 165 mg sodium; 31.3 g carbohydrate; 0.9 g dietary fiber; 8.8 g total sugars; 6.9 g protein.

Mini S'mores Tarts

A perfect way to celebrate your milestone is to serve your guests with these mini-chocolate ganache perched on sweet graham crust and topped with marshmallow topping. Refrigerate the crust with filling in the fridge for several hours until firm before placing on top with marshmallow topping.

Servings: 8

Ingredients

For the crust:

1 1/2 cup **graham cracker crumbs** from 10 full sheet graham crackers

6 tablespoons melted **unsalted butter**

1/3 cup **granulated sugar**

For the filling:

1 cup **heavy cream** or **heavy whipped cream**

1/4 cup cubed **unsalted butter**

12 ounces coarsely chopped **semi-sweet chocolate**

For the marshmallow topping:

1/2 cup **granulated sugar**

2 fresh **egg whites**

1 teaspoon **pure vanilla extract**

1/8 teaspoon **cream of tartar**

Directions

Preheat the oven at 350 degrees Fahrenheit.

For the crust:

Prepare the crust by grinding the graham crackers in a food processor to form into crumbs. If not using a blender or processor, crush them by placing in a plastic bag and roll with a rolling pin.

38

Mix in a medium bowl the melted butter, granulated sugar and graham cracker crumbs with a rubber spatula until incorporated and resembles like coarse meal.

Evenly press the crumbs into the tartlet pan until compact and tight.

Repeat with the rest of the crumbs and tartlet pan. Pre-bake for ten minutes and let cool.

For the filling:

Prepare the filling by combining the butter and chocolate in a large bowl.

Heat the heavy cream in a small saucepan on medium low, whisking often and bring mixture to a slow boil. Remove from heat as soon as it starts to boil.

Pour over the chocolate mixture and gently stir until both chocolate and butter have melted and the ganache is smooth.

Evenly fill the ganache into the prebaked crusts and chill for two hours up to one day until firm.

For the topping:

When ready to serve, prepare the topping by combining the egg whites, cream of tartar and ½ cup granulated sugar in a heatproof bowl of your electric mixer.

Place the bowl with the mixture over a saucepan with 2" of simmering water.

Whisk the mixture for 4 minutes until the egg whites are warmed through and the sugar has dissolved.

Transfer the bowl to your electric mixer with a whisk attachment and beat for four to five minutes on high until soft and glossy peaks are formed.

Stir in vanilla extract and beat on high until well blended.

Spread the marshmallow topping on top of chilled tartlets. If necessary toast the topping using a kitchen torch.

Enjoy!

Nutritional Information: 564 calorie; 27.5 g fat (15.4 g saturated fat); 39 mg cholesterol; 214 mg sodium; 75 g carbohydrate; 1.3 g dietary fiber; 47.7 g total sugars; 6.5 g protein

French Apple Tart

This apple tart looks complicated with its array of ingredients, but the truth is, the apricot glaze is not actually needed as it does not add much flavor to the already yummy taste of the tart with a thin layer of frangipane on the bottom of the pan. But if you want it for this recipe, it's up to you.

Servings: 10

Ingredients

1 1/4 cups **flour**

Additional **flour** for dusting

12 tablespoons cubed and chilled **unsalted butter**, divided

1 tablespoon **sugar** (optional)

1/4 cup **sugar**

5 to 7 **apples** (Honey Crisp, Fuji, or Pink Lady)

1/4 teaspoon **table salt**

For the frangipane (optional):

2 tablespoons **sugar**

1/2 cup **almond flour**

2 tablespoons **butter** at room temperature

Pinch **salt**

2 teaspoons **vanilla** or **bourbon, brandy** or **rum**

1 small **egg**

For finishing:

Whipped cream or **vanilla ice cream**

1/2 cup **apricot jam**, optional

Directions

Peel and core the apples and cut into halves.

Make the pastry by combining in a food processor the flour, 8 tablespoons butter, sugar and salt. Pulse for ten times until resembles pea-size crumbles.

Sprinkle with three tablespoons of ice-cold water; pulse until moistened for three to four times, but not overdoing it.

Place the dough on a work surface and shape into a disk. To make ahead, wrap the dough in plastic wrap and chill up to three days.

Flatten the dough with a rolling pin to form into 13-inch circle and place in an 11-inch tart pan with detachable bottom. Trim the overhang and refrigerate for one hour.

Don't wash the bowl of your food processor and use it to combine the almond flour, egg, butter, and salt; pulse until combined.

Add the vanilla or substitute with rum, bourbon or brandy. Pulse until the mixture is smooth.

Heat the oven at 375 degrees F.

Evenly spread about two tablespoons of optional frangipane across the bottom of the tart shell in a thin layer.

Thinly slice one apple one at a time into sections, but not cutting through to form into a fan.

Gently press the slice apple fan and repeat with the fanned apple halves. Arrange the fanned apple half on the outer edge of the tart dough going inward. Repeat this process for the remaining seven fanned apple halves.

Separate the remaining slices and begin from the place where the apple halves touch. Work your way in and layer them to form a tight rose design, making sure to fill in gaps with the unused apples.

Dust with optional sugar and dot with butter. Bake for 60 to 70 minutes.

For the glaze, heat in a small saucepan the optional apricot jam until warmed through and strain into a bowl with a fine strainer.

Place the tarts to wire racks and brush directly the top with optional apricot glaze. Let cool, slice and serve with whipped cream.

Serve!

Nutritional Information: 314 calorie; 17.5 g fat (10.5 g saturated fat); 56 mg cholesterol; 180 mg sodium; 38.5 g carbohydrate; 4.4 g dietary fiber; 21 g total sugars; 2.9 g protein.

Strawberry Kiwi Tartlets

These mind-blowing tartlets will change the course of your family's dinner habit with its awe-inspiring taste. The tangy crust is a blend of lemon shortbread cookies, sugar and butter. It is paired with a tangy kiwi curd filling and topped with strawberries.

Servings: 6 small tartlets or 1 9-inch tart

Ingredients

For the crust:

6 tablespoons melted **unsalted butter**

2 tablespoons **sugar**

7 ounces **lemon shortbread cookies** or **vanilla cookies**

For the kiwi curd:

1/2 cup **sugar**

3/4 cup **kiwi puree** (from 3 to 4 kiwi fruit)

3 **egg yolks**

3 **eggs**

6 tablespoons **unsalted butter**, cut into cubes

1 1/2 tablespoons **Meyer lemon juice**

Green food coloring, optional

Strawberries, for garnish

Directions

Preheat the oven at 375 degrees F.

Pulse in a food processor the cookies until it becomes a powder of about 1 ½ cups crumb. Add the sugar and melted butter; pulse until moistened.

Press the mixture into one 9" tart pan or six 3 ¾" tartlet pans. Bake for four to five minutes until lightly golden. If the crust tends to puff,

45

gently press the bottom back to its original place with a spoon. Let cool.

Prepare the kiwi curd by straining the kiwi puree with a fine mesh sieve into a bowl. Reserve the kiwi seeds.

Combine in a medium saucepan with heavy bottom the kiwi puree, lemon juice and sugar.

Meanwhile, beat the 3 eggs and 3 egg yolks together and stir in kiwi mixture.

Stir in butter on medium low heat for ten to fifteen minutes until the curd has thickened and the butter has melted, making sure it does not reach boiling point.

Stir in optional green food coloring.

Press the kiwi curd through a fine strainer to remove any egg bits or lumps. You may also add the reserved kiwi seeds to the curd, stir to evenly coat.

Fill the crusts with curd, chill for 1 to 2 hours until set.

Garnish with strawberry slices.

Enjoy!

Nutritional Information: 592 calorie; 36 g fat (21.6 g saturated fat); 269 mg cholesterol; 196 mg sodium; 52.1 g carbohydrate; 2.7 g dietary fiber; 42.9 g total sugars; 6 g protein.

THE ULTIMATE LEMON TART

Give an overhaul of Tiramisu by preparing it in a different way. This time serve it in tart form. There is no doubt that diners will embrace its delicious crust and creamy filling, that are both flavored with lemon zest. Your effort in prebaking the crust and preparing the ingredients is rewarded in the end.

Servings: 2 x 28cm tarts (10 slices)

Ingredients

For the sweet short crust pastry:

9 ounces cubed **cold butter**

4 cups **flour**

1 cup **icing sugar**

Zest of 1 lemon

2 **egg yolks**

3 to 4 tablespoons **ice water**

For the filling:

2 cups **cream**

2 1/2 cups **sugar**

9 **extra-large free range eggs**

1 cup **lemon juice**

Zest of 2 lemons

Directions

Combine in a bowl of your food processor the lemon zest, flour, icing sugar and butter. Pulse until it looks like rough bread crumbs.

Stir in egg yolks while the processor is running; add the water in spoonfuls until the dough turns into a ball.

Place the dough on a flour surface and form into two discs. Wrap the discs in plastic wrap and chill for fifteen minutes.

Preheat the oven at 356°F.

Remove the pastry dough from fridge and roll out on the surface. Press into prepared 2by28cm tart cases and blind bake for ten minutes. Remove the baking paper and the baking beans.

Return the half-baked pastry to the oven and bake for ten minutes more. Remove and let cool while preparing the filling.

Reduce oven heat to 212 degrees F.

Prepare the filling by heating the sugar and cream in a saucepan until tiny bubbles show around the edges of the pan, but not reaching boiling point.

Whisk the eggs in a separate bowl.

Slowly add the hot cream into the eggs while whisking. Stir in lemon zest and lemon juice until well blended.

Strain directly into a jug and then pour into the prebaked tart cases.

Bake for fifty minutes until the edges have firmed up, but the center is a bit jiggly. Remove baked tart from oven, let cool completely before refrigerating for several hours.

When serving, slice the tart and sprinkle with icing sugar.

Serve!

Nutritional Information: 716 calorie; 29.5 g fat (16.8 g saturated fat); 273 mg cholesterol; 234 mg sodium; 104.2 g carbohydrate; 1.9 g dietary fiber; 64.2 g total sugars; 12.4 g protein.

CANNOLI TART

Would you believe that this delectable tart is not what you think of? Though it looks so sweet with its sugary content, it is not so sweet at all. With the right amount of ingredients, it reduces the sweetness of the tart. You can indulge a slice of this tart without worrying too much about your dietary restrictions.

Servings: 6

Ingredients

For the crust:

½ cups **sugar**

Additional 1 tablespoon **sugar**

2 cups **sifted flour**

1 teaspoon **cinnamon**

½ teaspoons **salt**

⅓ cups **cold butter**

1 tablespoon **milk**

1 **whole egg**

For the filling:

1 **whole egg**

2 ¼ cups **ricotta**

2 teaspoons **amaretto**

2 teaspoons **sugar**

½ cups **chocolate chips** or **chunks**

Directions

For the crust:

Place in a food processor the flour, cinnamon, salt and sugar; pulse several times.

Add the butter to the mixture, pulse until it forms pea-sized crumbles. Stir in milk and egg; pulse again until it forms a large ball.

If you prefer mixing it by hand, combine the flour, cinnamon, salt and sugar and whisk several times to incorporate. Cut in the butter to form the mixture into pea-sized crumbles. Combine the milk and egg with your hands; knead into a ball.

Now, put the dough ball in between two sheets of parchment paper and roll out to fit into a deep dish tart or pie pan.

Coat the pan with oil or nonstick cooking spray and place the dough. Chill while preparing the filling and the oven is preheating at 350 degrees F.

For the filling:

Combine in a hand mixer or food processor the egg, amaretto, sugar and ricotta.

Add the chocolate chips and stir to blend. Pour the filling into the preheated crust.

Bake for twenty-five to thirty-five minutes until the filling is slightly puffed up and the crust is golden browned.

Sprinkle on top with powdered sugar or chocolate.

Enjoy!

Nutritional Information: 430 calorie; 23.3 g fat (14.5 g saturated fat); 114 mg cholesterol; 546 mg cholesterol; 41 g carbohydrate; 1 g dietary fiber; 29.4 g total sugars; 14.7 g protein.

Malted Chocolate Mousse Tart

This rock star tart is simple to prepare by grinding up the Oreo into fine crumbs, coat it with butter and press into tart pans before refrigerating until set. Prepare the whipped cream and chocolate mousse and fold them together before filling in the tart. Pipe the remaining whipped cream around the edges of tart.

Servings: 12-16 slices

Ingredients

For the crust:

1 (14.3 ounces) package **Oreos**

1/2 cup (1 stick) **unsalted butter**

For the filling:

1 (8 ounces) package **cold cream cheese**

2 ounces **milk** or **dark chocolate chips**

½ cup **chocolate malt powder**

1 tablespoon **unsalted butter**

1 1/4 cup **heavy whipping cream**

2 tablespoons of **heavy whipping cream**

½ cup **granulated sugar**

1/2 cup **powdered sugar**

2 to 4 ounces chopped **chocolate bar**

Directions

Grind up in a food processor the Oreos to form into a fine crumb.

Place the butter in a small microwave safe bowl. Microwave for thirty to forty-five seconds and pour into the crumbs until fully coated.

Press the Oreo crumbs into the bottom and up to the sides of the tart pan using a spatula. Chill until ready to use.

Beat cold cream cheese on medium speed for two minutes until fluffy and light, scraping down the sides of the bowl.

Combine in a small microwave-safe bowl the 1 tablespoon butter and chocolate chips. Microwave for thirty to sixty seconds and stir until smooth and melted.

Pour the mixture over the cream cheese, stir to combine well. Stir in the granulated sugar and malt powder. Beat the mixture on moderate speed until well blended.

Stir in two tablespoons of heavy whipping cream. Beat for two minutes on high speed to introduce extra air into the mousse.

To prepare the whip cream, place in the freezer a metal mixing bowl until cold for five to ten minutes.

Fill the chilled bowl with the heavy whipping cream. Beat using your electric mixer on medium high speed until thickened.

Gently add the powdered sugar and beat on high speed until it forms a stiff peak.

Fold one cup of the whipped cream gently into the chocolate mousse until incorporated and fill the tart shell.

Using a large-sized open star tip, pipe the remaining whipped cream around the edges of the tart. Chill for two to four hours until the mousse has firmed up.

When ready to serve, chop the chocolate bar into slivers and place on top of the tart.

Serve!

Nutritional Information: 386 calorie; 26.8 g fat (16.6 g saturated fat); 69 mg cholesterol; 190 mg sodium; 34.1 g carbohydrate; 0.4 g dietary fiber; 29.5 g total sugars; 4.5 g protein.

No-Bake Strawberry Chocolate Tart

This tart is addicting and one slice is not enough to satisfy your sweet cravings. You can always prepare this anytime as this does not require an oven to prepare. Grind up the Oreos in your food processor and with butter; press the crumb into the tart pan. Fill it with chocolate filling and garnish with strawberry and optional chopped nuts of your choice.

Servings: 10-12

Ingredients

For the Crust:

32 pieces **Oreo cookies**

1/2 cup **melted butter**

For the Chocolate filling:

7 ounces **milk chocolate**

3.5 ounces **bittersweet chocolate**

7 ounces **heavy cream**

Topping:

10 ounces fresh **strawberries**

Chopped **assorted nuts** (optional)

Directions

In the bowl of a food processor, place the Oreo and blend until it forms into fine crumbs. Stir in melted butter and process until the crumbs are moistened.

Press the mixture into the bottom up to the sides of a rectangular 5"by14" tart pan. Use the back of a spoon to press until compact. Freeze for a few minutes, while preparing the filling.

Place the heavy cream in a saucepan and heat on medium low for a few minutes, do not bring to a simmer or boil.

Remove immediately from heat and pour into chopped chocolate. Let it rest for one to two minutes, stirring until melted.

Pour the chocolate filling on top of Oreo crust.

Garnish on top with fresh strawberries and optional chopped nut.

Chill for two hours or overnight.

Serve!

Nutritional Information: 470 calorie; 32.8 g fat (18.1 g saturated fat); 56 mg cholesterol; 243 mg sodium; 42.3 g carbohydrate; 2.9 g dietary fiber; 27.4 g total sugars; 3.9 g protein.

RASPBERRY CURD TART

This stunning tart is ideal for celebrating a milestone. You can make ahead for the tart shell and the filling just place them in the fridge for the upcoming celebration. It is simply prepared by filling the tart shell with raspberry curd and top with lemon curls and raspberries.

Servings: 1 14-inch tart, 12 servings

Ingredients

Raspberry curd:

1/2 cup **sugar**

3 cups **raspberries**

2 tablespoons **Meyer lemon juice**

1 teaspoon **Meyer lemon zest**

2 large **egg yolks**

1 tablespoon chilled diced **unsalted butter**

2 tablespoons **water**

1/8 teaspoon **salt**

2 tablespoons plus 2 teaspoons **cornstarch**

Crust:

1/4 cup sliced toasted and finely **ground almonds**

7 tablespoons **unsalted butter**

1 1/4 cups **flour**

1/4 teaspoon **salt**

1/4 cup **sugar**

Topping:

Lemon peel curls (optional)

1 cup **raspberries**

Directions

Prepare the curd:

Combine in a saucepan the raspberries, lemon juice, lemon zest, water and sugar on medium high heat. Let boil for five minutes and simmer on low for five minutes. Remove saucepan from heat; let stand for five minutes.

When cooled, place the raspberry mixture in a food processor; process until the texture is smooth. Strain with a fine mesh strainer directly into a bowl. Discard the lumps.

Wipe the saucepan with paper towel and pour the strained raspberry mixture.

Whisk in a small bowl the cornstarch and egg yolks until smooth and stir directly into the raspberry mixture. Bring to a boil for five minutes on medium low heat. Cook and stir for 1 minute and remove from heat when thickened.

Gently stir in butter and salt until smooth.

Transfer the curd into a medium-sized bowl and cover with plastic wrap. Press the wrap directly onto the curd to avoid skin formation.

Refrigerate for two hours to a week if making ahead.

Prepare the crust:

Preheat the oven at 350°Fahrenheit.

Coat with nonstick spray a 14-inch rectangular tart pan with removable bottom.

Whisk in a medium bowl, the ground almonds, flour, salt and sugar.

Place the butter in a saucepan and cook on medium heat; stir often until foamy, and then clear and then turns into deep brown color for six minutes.

Fold the brown butter in flour mixture until incorporated. Press the mixture into the bottom up to the sides of the tart pan.

Bake the crust for twenty-four minutes until lightly golden. Let cool completely on wire rack.

To assemble the tart, fill the cooled tart shell with a spoonful of raspberry curd. Spread it evenly using an offset spatula.

Neatly arrange the raspberries on top of filling. Refrigerate for two hours.

Serve!

Nutritional Information: 240 calorie; 9.5 fat (5.7 g saturated fat); 55 mg cholesterol; 86 mg sodium; 30.1 g carbohydrate; 3.4 g dietary fiber; 20.6 g total sugars; 2.9 g protein.

Dulce de Leche Swirled Tarts

Both kids and adults cannot ignore the creamylicious multicolored tarts which are the result of swirling three different kinds of filling with a toothpick. The dark and white chocolate adds a magic touch to the dulce de leche that is snuggled on the crisp and fragrant not-so-sweet chocolate shell infused with cocoa flavor.

Servings: 8

Ingredients

For the chocolate tart dough:

1/4 cup **powdered sugar**

1 1/4 cups **all-purpose flour**

1/4 teaspoon **salt**

1/4 cup **unsweetened cocoa powder**

4 ounces cubed **cold unsalted butter**

1 **egg yolk**

For the dulce de leche filling:

1 can of **sweetened condensed milk**

12 ounces finely chopped **white chocolate**

1/2 cup of **heavy cream**

1/2 cup plus 2 tablespoons of **heavy cream**, divided

1/4 teaspoon **salt**

2 tablespoons **unsalted butter**, at room temperature

2 1/2 ounces finely chopped **semi-sweet chocolate**

Directions
Make the chocolate tart dough:

61

Combine together in a food processor the flour, sugar, cocoa powder and salt; pulse quickly until incorporated. Add the cubed butter to the mixture; pulse until the size is as small as a pea.

Stir in egg yolk; pulse in five-second burst until the dough comes together. Remove dough from processor; lightly knead for a few times to incorporate extra cocoa powder and flour.

Wrap the dough in plastic wrap and chill for a few days if making it in advance.

When ready to use, coat four pieces 6" tart pans (with detachable bottom) with nonstick cooking spray.

Press the dough into the bottom of the pan, extending to the sides in a thin and even layer.

Place the tart shell for half an hour in the freezer.

Preheat the oven at 375 degrees F.

Spritz the surface of dough with nonstick cooking spray.

Press foil into the shells and place on top with dry beans or pie weights. Bake the shells for ten to twelve minutes. Slowly detach the foil and dry beans. Continue baking for seven to eight minutes until the tart puffs and become dry and aromatic. Let cool completely.

Prepare the dulce de leche filling:

Detach the paper wrapper of condensed milk can and place in a slow cooker filled with water, an inch above the can. Set the cooker on low heat; cover with lid and cook for eight to nine hours or overnight.

When cooked, remove the can from slow cooker and let cool completely.

In a medium-sized bowl, place the white chocolate. Pour half of the heavy cream into a saucepan; bring to a simmer on medium high and pour half of it into the chopped white chocolate. Let it rest for one minute to soften the white chocolate.

Whisk the hot cream and white chocolate until glossy and smooth. If there are chocolate chunks, microwave it in ten –second increments while whisking at the same time until melted thoroughly.

Add the salt and butter to the mixture, whisking to incorporate.

Separate ½ cup of the white chocolate filling in a small bowl, set aside while the remaining half is added to the dulce de leche and whisk until smooth.

Separate ½ cup of the dulce de leche filling while melting the semi-sweet chocolate in bowl.

Combine the melted chocolate with ½ cup dulce de leche, adding 2 tablespoons of cream to thin out the chocolate mixture. In this way, you have a large bowl of dulce de leche filling and a small bowl of white chocolate filling.

Fill the cooled tart shells with dulce de leche filling about half full. Top it with a small spoon, dollop small spoon of three fillings. Swirl it with a toothpick through the filling to form a marbled design.

Follow these steps for the remaining tart shells and fillings. Chill for one hour to set the filling.

When ready to serve, let the tarts sit at room temperature for half an hour for silky and soft filling result.

Serve!

Nutritional Information: 637 calorie; 36 g fat (22.1 g saturated fat); 93 mg cholesterol; 321 mg sodium; 72.3 g carbohydrate; 1.5 g dietary fiber; 54.4 g total sugars; 9.3 g protein.

Rustic Strawberry Peach Tart

A galette of this lovely tart would not be enough to satisfy your cravings because you want to ask for more. You just can't resist the temptation of eating a lot of slices as the tart is packed with mouthwatering strawberry and peaches filling that cushion on buttery crust.

Servings: 1 galette (4 slices)

Ingredients

Filling:

2 cups sliced **fresh strawberries**

2 peeled, pitted & sliced **fresh ripe peaches**

1 teaspoon **vanilla extract**

2 tablespoons **granulated sugar**

Crust:

3 tablespoons **granulated sugar**

1 1/2 cups **all-purpose flour**

1/2 cup (1 stick) cubed **cold unsalted butter**

1/4 teaspoon **salt**

1 **egg**, beaten for egg wash

1/4 cup **ice water**

Additional **sugar** for sprinkling

Directions

Make the crust:

Whisk in a medium bowl the flour, salt and sugar.

Cut in the butter with a pastry cutter until the mixture looks like coarse crumbs with a size of a pea.

Stir in ¼ cup ice water until the dry ingredients are moistened. If the dough still dry, add an extra tablespoon of ice water.

Knead the dough several times in the bowl until sticky. Form the dough into a ball, flat it into a thick disk and wrap in plastic wrap. Chill for one hour.

Preheat the oven at 425°Fahrenheit.

Cover the bottom of a large baking sheet with a silicone baking mat or parchment, set aside.

Roll the dough on a surface dusted lightly with flour and form into a twelve-inch circle. Trim the overhang and transfer the dough to the baking sheet.

Fill the center of the dough with solid fruit without the juice, leaving a two to three-inch allowance along its border.

Fold the edges on top of the fruit, and overlap. Seal by pressing the edges.

Pour on top of fruit with reserved juice. Reserve 1 to 2 tablespoons of juice to avoid soggy dough.

Using a pastry brush, coat the crust with beaten egg. Sprinkle on top with sugar.

Bake for 24 to 35 minutes until the crust is nicely brown. Remove tart from oven and let cool slightly.

Enjoy!

Nutritional Information: 502 calorie; 25 g fat (15 g saturated fat); 102 mg cholesterol; 328 mg sodium; 63.5 g carbohydrate; 3.9 g dietary fiber; 25.9 g total sugars; 7.6 g protein.

Twix Tart

It is 100% guaranteed that your loved ones will love the taste of these Twix Tart, which uses a shortbread crust as base and top it with a chewy caramel filling. Layered on top of the filling is the milk chocolate ganache, which is a blend of heavy cream and milk chocolate.

Servings: 6 to 8

Ingredients

For the shortbread crust:

½ cup **powdered sugar**

1½ cups **all-purpose flour**

1 lightly beaten **egg**

9 tablespoons **chilled unsalted butter**, cut into ½-inch cubes

¼ teaspoon **salt**

For the caramel filling:

4½ tablespoons **sweetened condensed milk**

½ cup plus 1 teaspoon **heavy cream**

6 tablespoons **Lyle's golden syrup**

½ cup **granulated sugar**

2 tablespoons room temperature **unsalted butter**, cut into small pieces

2 tablespoons **water**

For the milk chocolate ganache:

5 tablespoons **heavy cream**

7 ounces finely chopped **milk chocolate**

Directions
Make the Shortbread Crust:

Place in a food processor the flour, sugar and salt and pulse. Scatter on top with butter pieces and pulse until the texture resembles coarse sand. Pulse 5 to 10 times if the butter is larger than pea size.

Add the egg in batches; pulse every addition and process for ten seconds after the eggs are added, until the texture resembles large clumps.

Transfer the dough in a 13 ¾" by 4 ¼" rectangular tart pan. Press to form an even layer on the bottom and up to the sides of the pan.

Roll the topmost part of the tart pan to remove excess batter. Freeze for half an hour.

Preheat oven at 375 degrees Fahrenheit.

Prick the dough with fork, cover with foil and press tightly against the cold crust to cover the sides.

Transfer the tart pan on a baking sheet. Bake for twenty to twenty-five minutes until lightly browned.

Gently remove the foil. Press the tart if it puffs up using the back of a spoon. Bake again for ten to fifteen minutes more until golden brown.

Remove sheet from oven and transfer the tart pan to cooling rack to fully cool.

Make the Caramel Filling:

Combine the sweetened condensed milk and heavy cream in a small saucepan on low heat. Stir often until the milk is melted and mixed with the cream. Remove from stove, cover to keep warm.

Mix in a medium-sized saucepan the water, golden syrup and sugar; warm on low heat, stir often until the sugar has melted.

Cook on medium heat undisturbed until the syrup is reached at 250 degrees F if measured on an instant-read thermometer. Remove immediately from heat.

Stir in the butter and incorporate the cream mixture in a gentle fashion to prevent the caramel from producing bubbles.

Return to the stove on medium heat, cook and stir often until the thermometer reading reaches at 240 degrees F.

Fill the shortbread crust with the hot caramel, let cool and set for thirty minutes.

Prepare the Milk Chocolate Ganache:

Put the chopped chocolate in a small bowl, set aside.

Pour the heavy cream in a saucepan; bring to a quick simmer on moderate heat and add the chopped chocolate. Let stand for two minutes; stir until smooth.

Spread in an even layer the milk chocolate ganache on top of caramel layer.

Chill the tart for thirty minutes or more to let the ganache set. Let the cold tart sit for 20 minutes at room temperature before serving.

Slowly remove the tart from the pan and slice. If there are leftovers, wrap them in plastic wrap and refrigerate for up to five days.

Serve!

Nutritional Information: 809 calorie; 46 g fat (28 g saturated fat); 131 mg cholesterol; 148 mg sodium; 97 g carbohydrate; 2 g dietary fiber; 69 g total sugars; 7 g protein.

Summer Berry Tart

Include in your list this summery tart filled with creamy filling, which is an assortment of double cream, Crème Fraiche, meringue nests, optional rum, vanilla bean seeds and icing sugar. Fresh ripe mixed seasonal berries are garnish on top of filling.

Servings: 8

Ingredients

1.3 pounds **mixed seasonal berries**

4 broken **meringue nests**

1 cup **double cream**

½ cup **Crème Fraiche**

¼ cup **icing sugar**

1 **Vanilla bean** seeds scraped out

1 tablespoon **rum** (optional)

For the tart:

2 cups **flour** plus extra for dusting

¼ cup **icing sugar**

4 ounces cubed **unsalted butter**

1 large **egg**

A little splash of **milk**

Butter for greasing the tart tin

Directions

Prepare the tart:

Combine in a large bowl the icing sugar and flour. Stir in cubed butter and mix again until the mixture bears a resemblance to coarse crumbs.

Stir in a splash of milk to let the dough come together and turn into a ball. Cover with a plastic wrap. Freeze for half an hour.

Sprinkle the rolling pin and your work surface with flour.

Roll the dough out on the work surface in a big size enough to fit in a 9-inch tart tin with a loose bottom. Coat the tart tin with butter.

Drape the dough on top of the rolling pin and then place it into the tart tin and up to the sides. Remove extra bits.

Pierce the dough with a fork all over. Cover the tart with plastic wrap and freeze for 30 minutes.

Preheat your oven at 350 degrees Fahrenheit.

Remove the tart dough from the freezer and line the bottom with parchment paper. Push it into the side and fill the tart with baking beans or baking rice. Blind bake the tart for ten minutes.

Remove tart from oven, and remove the baking beans or baking rice and parchment paper. Bake for another ten minutes until golden and firm. Let cool before adding the filling.

Always see to it that blind baking step is the first thing you do to thwart the tart shell from shrinking.

Prepare the filling by whipping the crème fraîche and double cream with vanilla bean seeds, rum and icing sugar until the smooth and soft peaks are formed.

Add the broken meringue nest. Spoon the filling into the tart shell.

Garnish with mixed berries.

Serve!

Nutritional Information: 467 calorie; 25 g fat (15.1 g saturated fat); 95 mg cholesterol; 149 mg sodium; 54.7 g carbohydrate; 2 g dietary fiber; 23.1 g total sugars; 6.7 g protein.

Salted Caramel Bittersweet Chocolate Tart

The sweet tart is filled with a creamy and chocolaty filling, which is a blend of heavy whipping cream, whole milk, egg and bittersweet chocolate. The filling is topped with caramel and flecked with sea salt, not iodized salt.

Servings: One 10" tart (8 slices)

Ingredients

Sweet pastry dough:

1½ tablespoons **granulated sugar**

1¼ cups **all-purpose flour**

7 tablespoons **cold butter**, cut into ¼" pieces

¼ teaspoon **salt**

½ teaspoon **vanilla bean** or **vanilla extract**

1 **egg yolk**

2½ tablespoons **ice water**

For the filling:

½ cup **whole milk**

¾ cup **heavy whipping cream**

1 **egg yolk**

1 **egg**

12 ounces chopped **bittersweet chocolate**

For the salted caramel:

6 tablespoons room temperature **salted butter**

1 cup **granulated sugar**

1 teaspoon **salt**

½ cup room temperature **heavy whipping cream**

Directions

Prepare the dough:

Whisk in a large bowl the flour, salt and sugar.

Whisk in another bowl the vanilla, egg yolk and ice water and slowly pour into the dry ingredients. Mix until incorporated.

Cut the cold butter into the flour-egg mixture using a pastry blender until it looks like pea-size clumps.

Knead into a ball, press slightly to flatten and wrap with a sheet of plastic wrap. Chill for one hour.

Roll the dough into a 1/8-inch thick circle and fit into a removable bottomed-tart pan. Trim excess dough and place an aluminum foil on top.

Place a pie weight on top of foil and bake for twenty minutes at 325 degrees F until lightly golden brown in color. Let cool and set aside.

Prepare the filling:

Pour the whole milk and heavy cream into a medium-sized saucepan.

Heat the mixture on medium heat until boiling; remove from heat. Stir in chopped bittersweet chocolate until smooth.

Whisk in another bowl the eggs and stir in ¼ of the milk chocolate mixture while whisking vigorously until combined well, but not scrambled.

Pour the mixture into the pan and whisk to combine well. Fill the tart with the filling and bake for 25 to 30 minutes until set at 325 degrees F.

Prepare the salted caramel:

Pour the granulated sugar into a small saucepan and heat on medium; stir often to prevent burning.

Add the salted butter to the melted sugar; stir frequently for one to two minutes until the butter has totally melted.

Add the ice cream and boil for one minute. Remove from heat. Stir in salt. Let cool for fifteen minutes.

When the tart is cooled, gently pour the caramel. Chill for 2 hours.

Garnish with sea salt.

Enjoy!

Nutritional Information: 769 calorie; 40.9 g fat (26 g saturated fat); 160 mg sodium; 495 mg sodium; 92.7 g carbohydrate; 2.6 g dietary fiber; 56.2 g total sugars; 10.1 g protein.

Chocolate Salted Caramel Tart

Be mystified by the magic of this gooey tart made with the goodness of almond chocolate sweet pastry. Atop the chocolate crust is the chocolaty salted caramel. The bittersweet chocolate ganache is spread over caramel and garnished with sea salt crystals.

Servings: 6-8

Ingredients

Almond Chocolate Sweet Pastry:

1/4 cup **ground almonds**

1 1/4 cups **flour**

1/4 teaspoon **salt**

1/4 cup **sugar**

1/4 cup **unsweetened cocoa powder**

110 g **cold unsalted butter,** cut into small (1/2-inch) cubes

1 **egg**

1 teaspoon **vanilla extract**

1 to 2 tablespoon **ice water**

For the caramel:

1/2 cup **water**

1 1/2 cups **sugar**

1 teaspoon **salt**

5 tablespoons **unsalted butter**

1/2 cup **heavy cream**

Chocolate Ganache:

4 ounces chopped **bittersweet chocolate**

1/2 cup **heavy cream**

Garnish:

Flecks of **sea salt crystals**

Directions

Preheat the oven at 350 degrees F.

Make the sweet pastry:

Combine in a large bowl the flour, cocoa powder, ground almonds, salt and sugar.

Cut the butter with a pastry blender into the mixture until it forms crumbs. Add the vanilla extract and egg, and then the water and mix to incorporate well.

Wrap the dough with a sheet of plastic. Slowly knead to form a disc and chill for 30 minutes longer.

Roll the dough on a flour surface or on top of the plastic wrap to form into a circle, 1 ½" bigger than the tart pan.

Transfer the dough to a prepared greased nine-inch tart pan. Remove the overhang edges. Chill for half an hour.

Pierce the dough using a fork and place a parchment paper on top. Spread the dry beans on the paper or pie weights.

Bake for fifteen minutes.

Remove the beans and parchment paper; return pan to the oven and bake for ten to fifteen minutes. Let cool completely.

Make the caramel:

In a heavy bottomed saucepan, cook the water and sugar on medium high heat, undisturbed until the sugar is caramelized.

Remove saucepan from heat and stir in cream until it produce bubbles. Cook for one to two minutes, stir with a wooden spoon until the mixture is smooth.

Remove saucepan from heat and stir in salt and butter. Stir often until the mixture is smooth, slightly cool and pour into the chocolate crust.

Chill for 4 to 5 hours until set.

Make the chocolate ganache:

Pour the heavy cream into a small saucepan and heat until the edges start to boil.

Remove the saucepan from heat and pour into the chopped chocolate. Let stand for 1 minute; stir until the chocolate is dissolved.

Pour the chocolate ganache on top of the caramel, spreading evenly. Refrigerate for two to three hours.

Fleck with sea salt crystals.

Serve!

Nutritional Information: 557 calorie; 30.4 g fat (18.4 g saturated fat); 93 mg cholesterol; 489 mg sodium; 69.7 g carbohydrate; 2.3 g dietary fiber; 51.4 g total sugars; 5.4 g protein.

Raspberry Chocolate Tart

Your friends will get stunned by the awesomeness of this tart with raspberries lined in even rows and dusted with powdered sugar. The flaky creamy tart shell is loaded with buttery chocolate ganache filling. It is perfect for your weekend get-together!

Servings: 7-8 slices

Ingredients

For the crust:

1/2 cup **confectioner's sugar**

1 1/2 cups **all-purpose flour**

1(4 1/2 ounces) stick plus 1 tablespoon frozen **unsalted butter**, cut into small pieces

1 lightly beaten large **egg**

1/4 teaspoon **salt**

For the chocolate ganache filling:

¾ cup **cream**

8 ounces chopped **bittersweet chocolate**

2 tablespoons **butter**

2 teaspoons **vanilla**

For the topping:

Powdered sugar for dusting

2 pints fresh **raspberries**

Directions

Make the Crust:

Put together in a bowl of your food processor the confectioner's sugar, flour and salt; pulse several times until incorporated.

Add in the butter; pulse until incorporated with some pieces resembles a pea size while other look like oatmeal flakes.

Gently add the egg and pulse at the same time. Process a few times until the dough comes together.

Transfer the dough on a silicon mat and knead several times until sticky.

Press into the bottom of oiled tart pan with detachable bottom. Make sure to press up to the sides of tart shell and pierce the dough a few times with a fork. Place in the freezer for half an hour or more.

Preheat the oven at 375 degrees Fahrenheit.

Coat a piece of aluminum foil with butter and place in the crust with buttered side downward.

Place in oven and bake for twenty to twenty-five minutes.

Gently remove the foil, pressing down the crust when it has puffed up using the back of your spoon.

Bake for another ten minutes until golden brown and firm. Let cool.

Make the Chocolate Ganache Filling:

Put the bittersweet chocolate in a heatproof bowl.

In a small saucepan on low heat, place the vanilla and cream, stirring frequently until slightly simmering.

Pour the cream into the chocolate, whisking until smooth and melted.

Stir in butter and whisk until glossy and smooth.

Pour into the tart shell and evenly spread. Let ganache set for ten minutes without touching.

Arrange the fresh raspberries on top of the chocolate ganache filling in even rows or four each row.

Sprinkle on top with powdered sugar.

Enjoy!

Nutritional Information: 529 calorie; 28.3 g fat (19.3 g saturated fat); 82 mg cholesterol; 127 mg sodium; 61 g carbohydrate; 7.6 g dietary fiber; 22.5 g total sugars; 7.4 g protein.

Rustic Cherry Tarts

These gorgeous sweet cherries are perched on a flaky crust. The filling is naturally sweetened by the sweet cherries, so nothing to worry if you think you can consume two tarts. It is so simple to prepare and it is best to serve fresh from the oven.

Servings: 4 - 6 Inch Tarts

Ingredients

For the Crust:

3/4 teaspoon **salt**

1 1/2 cup **all-purpose flour**

1/4 cup **ice cold water**

1/2 cup **shortening**

2 tablespoons **sugar**

For the filling:

3 tablespoons **sugar**

4 cups pitted **sweet cherries**

1 beaten **egg**

1 1/2 teaspoons **cornstarch**

Directions

In a medium bowl, mix together the flour, salt and sugar.

Cut in shortening with a pastry blender until pea sized crumbs.

Splash the mixture with cold water, stirring lightly with a fork until it forms into a ball. Refrigerate for 1 hour or longer until firmed up.

Preheat the oven at 400 degrees F.

Combine the cherries, cornstarch and sugar. Divide the dough into four parts and roll out into an eight-inch circle, trimming overhang edges.

Fill the center of each circle with a cup of sweet cherries, making sure to leave 1 ½ inch allowance around the crust edges.

Fold the edge over the cherries and make a pleat. Brush the tart crust with beaten egg.

Bake for twenty-five to thirty minutes until the cherries are tender and the crust is nicely golden.

Serve!

Nutritional Information: 552 calorie; 26.7 g fat (7.9 g saturated fat); 0 mg cholesterol; 447 mg sodium; 73.8 carbohydrate; 4.3 g dietary fiber; 34.2 g total sugars; 7.7 g protein.

ROASTED CHERRY CHOCOLATE TART

You can tell the amazing taste of this tart with its juicy-tender roasted cherry toppings and whipped cream place on top of each other. The tart shell is overloaded with ingredients to come up with rich chocolate and creamy texture, amongst them are Dutch-process cocoa powder, butter, flour, cream, sugar, egg and vanilla.

Servings: 8

Ingredients

For the tart shell:

1 tablespoon **heavy cream**

1 large **egg yolk**

1 cup **all-purpose flour**

1/2 teaspoon **vanilla extract**

2/3 cup **confectioners' sugar**

¼ cup **Dutch-process cocoa powder**

8 tablespoons cold **unsalted butter**, cut into 1/2-inch cubes

1/4 teaspoon **salt**

For the filling:

3 to 4 tablespoons **sugar**

1 teaspoon **vanilla extract**

4 cups fresh **pitted and halved cherries**

3 tablespoons **confectioners' sugar**

1 cup **heavy cream**

To finish:

Chocolate syrup (optional)

Directions

Make the tart shell:

Whisk in a small bowl the egg yolk, vanilla and heavy cream. Set aside.

Pulse in a food processor the cocoa powder, flour, salt and sugar until well combined.

Spread the pieces of butter on top of flour mixture. Process in 1-second pulses to cut the butter into the flour-cocoa mixture until it looks like coarse meal. You can also use a stand mixer or a pastry cutter to do this step.

Add the egg mixture while the processor is running; process until the dough is easy to handle for about twelve seconds.

Place the dough on a sheet of plastic wrap, pressing into a six-inch disc. Cover the dough in a sheet of plastic wrap. Chill for 1 hour or up to 2 days.

When ready to use, remove the dough from the fridge, unwrap and roll on a floured surface into a thirteen-inch round.

Place the dough in a 9" tart pan up to the sides and trim excess. Place the tart pan on a large plate and place in the freezer for half an hour.

Rearrange the oven rack to the center.

Preheat the oven at 375° Fahrenheit.

Place the tart pan on a baking sheet. Press a twelve-inch square of aluminum foil into the frozen tart shell up to the edge. Place pie weights on top. Bake for thirty minutes, making sure to rotate the sheet halfway through.

Remove the baking sheet. Remove the foil and pie weights. Bake again for five to eight minutes more until dark golden brown. Let cool on wire rack.

Adjust the oven temperature at 450 degrees F.

Mix together in your baking dish, the cherries and sugar, tossing to combine well. Bake for ten minutes until the cherries are slightly softened and juices are starting to come out. Let cool completely.

Meanwhile, combine in a bowl of your stand mixer with a whisk attachment, the confectioner's sugar and heavy cream.

Whip on moderate high speed until stiff peaks are formed. Stir in vanilla. Fill tart shell with 2/3 of the roasted cherries, spreading evenly.

Dot the whipped cream and spread evenly on top of cherries.

Put a spoonful of the remaining roasted cherries and place on top of whipped cream.

Drizzle with optional chocolate syrup on top of whipped cream. Chill for 1 hour longer.

Serve!

Nutritional Information: 346 calorie; 18.5 g fat (11.2 g saturated fat); 77 mg cholesterol; 180 mg sodium; 43.4 g carbohydrate; 2.4 g dietary fiber; 18.4 g total sugars; 3.4 g protein.

Maple Cream Tart

One of the highly recommended tarts for your sweet cravings is this recipe, which you have to make the tart shell from scratch, but it's worth rewarding. Perched on this buttery crust is the maple cream filling and top with a dollop of Creme fraîche or Greek yogurt.

Servings: 1 tart (8 slices)

Ingredients

Tart shell:

1 tablespoon **sugar**

1¼ **cups all-purpose flour**

¼ teaspoon **table salt**

8 tablespoons **unsalted butter**

¼ cup plus 1 tablespoon **ice water**

Maple cream filling:

1/4 cup **maple syrup**

1 cup **packed light brown sugar**

1/4 cup **all-purpose flour**

1 1/4 cups **heavy cream**

 Creme fraîche or **Greek yogurt**, for serving

Directions

For the shell:

Whisk in a mixing bowl the flour, salt and sugar.

Cut the butter with a pastry cutter until incorporated into the flour mixture and turn into small pieces.

Add a few drops of ice water and keep on stirring with fork until the mixture forms a mass.

Add more water little by little if necessary, until the mixture forms into a ball.

Cover with a sheet of plastic wrap and refrigerate for 30 minutes or overnight.

For the filling:

Roll out the dough into an eleven-inch circle and slowly place in a tart pan, pressing against the pan's bottom and up to the sides.

Pierce the dough with a fork and refrigerate for twenty minutes.

Heat the oven at 400 degrees F.

Place a parchment paper on top of tart dough and put pie weights or dried beans. Bake for twenty minutes.

Remove the pie weights and paper. Bake for five minutes longer until the bottom of the pan is dried out. Remove from oven, let cool.

Reduce oven temperature to 350 degrees.

Whisk in a medium-sized bowl the sugar, cream, flour and maple syrup until combined and pour into the cooled tart crust.

Bake for twenty to twenty-five minutes until the maple cream sets, but jiggles when shaken. Let cool completely.

Add a dollop of Greek yogurt or crème fraîche on top of filling.

Serve!

Nutritional Information: 393 calorie; 19.1 g fat (11.9 g saturated fat); 59 mg cholesterol; 176 mg sodium; 51.7 g carbohydrate; 0.6 g dietary fiber; 32.3 g total sugars; 5.8 g protein.

Sweet and Salty Pretzel Tart with Chocolate Ganache and Peanut Butter Swirl

Love this jaw dropping dessert composed of sweet and salty pretzel tart and topped with chocolate ganache and mouthwatering peanut butter swirl. To create the peanut butter swirl, drag the knife when pouring the warm peanut butter into the chocolate ganache.

Servings: 1 tart (8-10 slices)

Ingredients

Crust:

1/2 cup room temperature **unsalted butter**

1 1/2 cup crushed **pretzels**

3/4 cup **powdered sugar**

1 **egg**

1 1/2 cup **flour**

Filling:

2 tablespoons **unsalted butter**

8 ounces chopped **semisweet chocolate**

3/4 cup **heavy cream**

Swirl:

1/2 cup **smooth peanut butter**

Directions

Make the crust:

Beat in a large bowl of your electric mixer the butter, half of crushed pretzels and powdered sugar until creamy.

Add the flour, remaining half of pretzels and egg, with some pieces of pretzel whole for added crunchiness.

Shape the dough into a flat ball and cover with plastic wrap. Refrigerate for 1 hour or more.

Remove the dough from the fridge and let sit for several minutes until easy to handle.

Coat with butter a twelve-inch round fluted tart pan with detachable bottom.

Place the dough in between two large sheets of waxed paper. Roll out the dough into a 15" circle.

Press the dough in the center of the tart pan up to the corners and fold excess dough back on top of the side to create a double edge crust. The dough should be at the same level of the edge of your tart pan.

Prick the dough several times with a fork. Freeze for thirty minutes.

Preheat the oven at 375 degrees F and rearrange the oven rack in the middle of the oven.

Butter the smooth side of aluminum foil and fit into the interior of tart shell. Put the tart shell on a baking sheet. Bake for twenty to twenty-five minutes.

Take out the foil and bake for ten minutes until the edges of crust is golden brown. Let tart cool fully on a wire rack before adding the filling.

Make the ganache:

Prepare the ganache by chopping the chocolate in an oven heatproof bowl, set aside.

Mix together in a small saucepan the butter and cream; heat on medium. When it starts to boil, pour into the chocolate and cover for three to five minutes. Whisk until the chocolate melts and the texture resemble a smooth pudding.

Pour the ganache into the cooled tart shell. Level it with spatula.

Place the peanut butter in a microwave-safe bowl and microwave until runny.

Pour the warm peanut butter over the chocolate ganache and swirl with a knife to produce peanut butter swirls.

Refrigerate for ten to fifteen minutes until the filling is firmed up.

Enjoy!

Nutritional Information: 694 calorie; 37 g fat (18.7 g saturated fat); 74 mg cholesterol; 677 mg sodium; 84.4 g carbohydrate; 4.5 g dietary fiber; 29.5 g total sugars; 13.3 g protein.

COCONUT CREAM TARTS

You will end up licking your finger with the creamy goodness of these tarts. The shortbread crust is filled with coconut cream, which is a perfect union of coconut cream, whole milk, vanilla bean, sweetened shredded coconut, cornstarch, egg yolks and sugar with final touches of whipping cream on top.

Servings: 6 – 3 inch tarts, or 1 -10 inch tart

Ingredients

Shortbread crust:

1/3 cup **sugar**

1 1/4 cups **flour**

1/2 cup **butter**, cut into chunks

Pinch of **salt**

1 **egg yolk**

6 pieces 3" mini tart pans or 1 large 10" tart pan

Coconut cream:

1/4 cup **cream of coconut**

2 cups **whole milk**

1/2 **vanilla bean**, split

1/2 cup **sweetened shredded coconut**

1/4 cup **sugar**

4 large **egg yolks**

1 pinch of **salt**

1 tablespoon **cornstarch**

Topping:

Whipping cream

94

Directions

Prepare the crust:

Preheat your oven at 400 degrees F.

Place the flour, sugar and salt in your food processor for ten seconds.

Add the butter chunks; process until it resembles coarse crumbs.

Add the egg yolk to the mixture; process until thoroughly mixed.

If making mini tarts or tartlets, divide the mixture into six 3" tart pans and press into the molds with the center lower than the sides. Bake for twelve to fifteen minutes.

Prick with fork a few times to prevent puffing up. Take a closer look at them not to overcook.

If making a large tart, press the dough into a 10" tart pan with the sides higher than the center. Bake for fifteen to eighteen minutes and prick the tart.

Prepare the coconut cream:

Combine in a saucepan the coconut cream, shredded coconut, vanilla bean and milk and then bring to a simmer on medium heat.

Remove saucepan from heat and let sit for an hour.

Beat in a mixer the sugar, egg yolks, salt and cornstarch until the color is pale yellow and the texture is thick.

Reheat the milk mixture after 1 hour to warm thoroughly and gently pour into the mixer while running at medium speed.

When thoroughly mixed, pour the cream into a saucepan and cook on medium heat while continue whisking until boiling and thick.

If you like, strain the cream through a fine mesh sieve to discard the shredded coconut, but for a crunchy texture, leave it there. Let cool fully before filling it in the tarts. Stir well before doing it.

Assembly:

95

Scoop the cooled coconut cream into the center of cooled tart and top with the whipping cream. Repeat with the rest of tartlets if using mini tarts.

If using a large tart pan, pour the entire coconut cream to the pan.

Serve!

Nutritional Information: 462 calorie; 32.2 g fat (21 g saturated fat); 226 mg cholesterol; 221 mg sodium; 35.9 g carbohydrate; 1.2 g dietary fiber;12.5 g total sugars; 8.7 g protein.

Rustic Rhubarb, Almond, and Honey Tart

Making the rhubarb as your filling might be unique in the like that it is not commonly used compared to fruits. Make sure to align the rhubarb with the dough and almond paste, and dust it with sugar. Add extra sweet to the tart by drizzling baked tart with honey.

Servings: 1 large tart (12 slices)

Ingredients

For the almond paste:

6 tablespoons **sugar**

1 cup sliced **almonds**

1/4 teaspoon **fine sea salt**

1/4 cup **sweet rice flour**

2 small **eggs**

1 **egg** for brushing the tart

6 tablespoons softened **unsalted butter**

1/2 teaspoon of **almond extract**

1 teaspoon **vanilla extract**

For finishing the tart:

All-Butter Pie Dough

Oat flour for rolling the dough

5 to 6 medium stalks **rhubarb**, at least 14" long

4 tablespoons **honey** for drizzling

3 tablespoons **sugar** for sprinkling

Directions

Make the almond paste:

Combine in a food processor the almonds, rice flour, sugar and salt; process until the almonds turn into fine crumbs.

Add the almond extract, vanilla extract, eggs and softened butter; process until smooth and turns into a paste.

Cover the paste if it seems runny, and refrigerate for 20 to 30 minutes until set.

Prepare the tart:

Remove cold dough from fridge and let it stand for five minutes at room temperature until slightly softened.

Place the dough in between two sheets of lightly floured parchment paper.

Press the dough to flatten out and roll into 12by16-inch rectangle.

Remove the topmost parchment and lightly dust the dough with flour.

Replace the parchment paper and grasp the sandwiched dough with your hand and turn over.

Remove the new topmost parchment, flour it and roll. Cut off excess long bits, press onto the short bits and roll to cling. Trim the sides of rectangle to align. Chill for ten to twenty minutes until the butter is set.

Slip the dough into a baking sheet pan with the parchment paper still on.

Evenly spread the almond paste on top of dough, leaving a one inch border around it.

Slowly fold over the edges to create the crust. Refrigerate for thirty minutes.

Rearrange the oven rack in the lower 3rd part.

Preheat the oven at 400 degrees F.

Trim the stalks of rhubarb with the same length of the dough; cut into half lengthwise. Lay the rhubarb across the chilled dough.

Brush the borders of tart with beaten egg. Dust the crust and rhubarb with sugar.

Bake the tart for 30 to 35 minutes until the vegetable is tender and the almond paste is puffed and nicely golden. Remove tart from oven, let cool.

Drizzle with honey and slice into 12 rectangles.

Serve!

Nutritional Information: 243 calorie; 11.9 g fat (4.5 g saturated fat); 38 mg cholesterol; 80 mg sodium; 32.4 g carbohydrate; 2.1 g dietary fiber; 15.2 g total sugars; 4.2 g protein.

Coconut Lime Tarts

Most of the tart recipes have a long list of instructions, but this recipe is the opposite one. You don't need to tire yourself in making the tart shell because you can use a premade baked tart shell and fill it with lime curd coconut cream filling and finish it with the toppings of lime zest, toasted coconut and whipped coconut cream.

Servings: 12 tarts

Ingredients

12 **premade baked tart shells**

Lime curd cream filling:

3/4 cup **granulated sugar**

3 large **eggs**

Zest of 1 or 2 limes

1/2 cup **fresh lime juice**

3/4 cup **whipped coconut cream**

4 tablespoons cubed **unsalted butter**

Garnish:

Grated **lime zest**

1/4 cup **toasted coconut**

1 1/2 cup **whipped coconut cream**

Directions

Prepare the lime curd cream filling:

Whisk in a small pot the lime juice & zest, sugar and eggs until smooth. Cook and stir on medium heat for 4 to 5 minutes until thickened.

Remove pot from heat and stir in unsalted butter until thoroughly melted. Let cool and set aside.

Add whipped coconut cream when the curd has cooled.

Spoon the filling into the cooled tart shells and chill until firm.

Repeat these steps for the rest of the coconut cream, tarts and finish it by placing the toasted coconut and zest of lime on top.

Chill until ready for serving.

Enjoy!

Nutritional Information: 321 calorie; 25 g fat (18 g saturated fat); 54 mg cholesterol; 58 mg sodium; 22 g carbohydrate; 1 g dietary fiber; 13 g total sugars; 4 g protein.

LUXURIOUS NUTELLA TART

Nutella lovers will shout for joy with this tart that is packed with lots of Nutella. The tart is made of layers of buttery hazelnut tart shell, gooey filling composed of hazelnuts, chocolate chips and Nutella. Though the Nutella glaze is optional, its addition adds luster and sheen to your tart.

Servings: 1 9-inch tart (8 to 10 slices)

Ingredients

For the hazelnut tart shell:

1/2 teaspoon **vanilla extract**

1 large **egg**

1/2 cup **confectioners' sugar**

1/2 cup **toasted hazelnuts**

1/8 teaspoon **salt**

1 cup **all-purpose flour**

5 tablespoons chilled **unsalted butter**, cut into 1/4-inch pieces

For the filling:

2 teaspoons **granulated sugar**

1/4 cup coarsely chopped **hazelnuts**

1/3 cup **semisweet chocolate chips**

1/2 cup **heavy cream**

1 1/4 cup **Nutella**

2 tablespoons softened **unsalted butter**

For the glaze (optional):

1 tablespoon **whole milk**

2 tablespoon **Nutella**

Directions

For the hazelnut tart shell:

Whisk in a small bowl the vanilla and egg, set aside.

In a food processor, process the sugar and hazelnuts until pulverized for eight to ten seconds. Stir in salt and flour; pulse to incorporate.

Spread the pieces of butter on top of mixture; pulse for 15 times, until it is similar to coarse cornmeal.

Add the egg mixture while the machine is running, via the feed tube and keep on processing for 12 seconds until the dough sticks to the processor blade.

Transfer the dough to a sheet of plastic wrap. Flatten it out into a 6" disk and tightly wrap in plastic. Chill for one hour up to two days.

When ready to use, roll out the cold dough on a work surface to soften a bit for ten minutes.

Roll into an 11" circle on the floured counter and then roll around the rolling pin. Lift the dough up and slowly fit into a 9" tart pan with detachable bottom. Cut excess dough and use the scraps to patch the thin areas.

Place the tart pan on a large plate; freeze for half an hour.

Reposition the oven rack in the center and preheat the oven at 375 degrees F.

Set your tart pan on a large baking sheet. Place a foil on top of the frozen tart shell up to the edges and put pie weights on top.

Bake for thirty minutes until set and golden brown; make sure to rotate your baking sheet halfway through baking time. Slowly remove the pie weights and foil.

Bake for 5 to 10 minutes more until golden and totally baked. Let tart shell cool on the sheet on a wire rack.

For the filling:

In a medium nonstick pan on medium heat, place the sugar and hazelnuts; cook and stir for 1 minute until caramelized and the nuts are nicely golden.

Ladle the nuts from the pan into a small bowl to cool.

In a saucepan on medium high heat, bring the heavy cream to a quick simmer.

Turn off heat and stir in the butter and chocolate chips. Cover and let stand for two minutes until the chocolates are mostly melted. Mildly stir until smooth.

In case the mixture has lots of chocolate bits, reheat on the lowest heat in a slow fashion, whisking often until totally smooth.

Add the Nutella, stirring often, until smooth.

When the candied hazelnuts are cooled, sprinkle it on top of the tart shell, making sure to break up the clumps.

Evenly spread the chocolate filling on top of nuts. Cover with plastic wrap and chill for two hours or overnight.

When ready to use, remove the cover and pour the optional glaze, tilting the pan to spread evenly. Smooth out the glaze with a spatula.

When ready to serve, detach the exterior metal ring of tart pan and slide a spatula between the bottom of the pan and the tart and slide gently to a serving plate.

For the optional glaze:

Whisk in a bowl the milk and Nutella until dissolved. If there are bits of Nutella, microwave the mixture for ten seconds and whisk.

Enjoy!

Nutritional Information: 463 calorie; 30.6 g fat (13.1 g saturated fat); 60 mg cholesterol; 131 mg sodium; 42.6 g carbohydrate; 2.8 g dietary fiber; 27.5 g total sugars; 5.8 g protein.

Blackberry Tart Recipe

Taste the great flavor of this striking tart made from scratch. Perched on the baked crust shell is the tangy blackberry filling, which is a combo of butter, sugar, flour, lemon zest, lemon juice and butter. Fresh blackberries dot the filling and sprinkled with white sugar for extra sweetness.

Servings: 10

Ingredients

Tart shell:

1 9" or 9.5" **tart crust shell**

Blackberry filling:

1 cup **white sugar**

5 cups fresh **blackberries**

1 tablespoon of **lemon zest**

2 tablespoons of freshly squeezed **lemon juice**

 1/2 cup **all-purpose flour**

1 tablespoon thinly chopped **cold butter**

2 tablespoons **white sugar**

Directions

Preheat the oven at 400 degrees Fahrenheit.

Prebake a 9" or 9.5" tart crust at 400 degrees F for twenty to thirty minutes and slightly cool.

Toss in a large bowl 4 cups blackberries, ½ cup flour, and 1 cup sugar, 1 tablespoon of lemon zest and 2 tablespoons of lemon juice. Mix until well blended.

Spoon the blackberry filling into the cooled tart shell.

Spread on top the remaining one cup of blackberries.

Dust 1 to 2 tablespoons of white sugar on top of berries and top the berries with thinly chopped cold butter.

Place the tart on your rimmed baking sheet. Bake for thirty to forty minutes at 350 degrees Fahrenheit until bubbly.

In case the crust is very quick to brown, place on top of tart a sheet of aluminum foil.

Serve tart with vanilla ice cream.

Enjoy!

Nutritional Information: 162 calorie; 2.3 g fat (1.1 g saturated fat); 3 mg cholesterol; 13 mg sodium; 35.7 g carbohydrate; 4 g dietary fiber; 26.2 g total sugars; 1.9 g protein.

Simple Apple Crumble Tart

If you like tart, but hate to prepare it because of its complicated instructions, here is a recipe that is considered the easiest so far. Slices of Granny Smith apples are piled evenly on top of pie crust and top it with a mixture of brown sugar and cinnamon, and top it with crumbs of cold butter.

Servings: 8 slices

Ingredients

1 **pie crust**

5 peeled and sliced **Granny Smith apples**

Pinch of **salt**

1 teaspoon **cinnamon**

1/2 cup **light brown sugar**

Crumb:

1/2 cup **flour**

1/2 cup **light brown sugar**

1/4 cup **cold butter**

Directions

Preheat the oven at 400° F.

Prepare a 9" to 10" tart pan by lining it with the crust. Pinch along its rim to form the tart crust.

Evenly pile the apple slices in the crust.

Mix together in a bowl the cinnamon and brown sugar and then sprinkle over the apple slices.

Cut the cold butter with a pastry cutter in a bowl until it resembles coarse sand.

Shape into large crumbs using your clean hands. Sprinkle on top of the sugar & cinnamon mixture.

Bake for forty to forty-five minutes until nicely golden crust and lightly browned top. Let cool before slicing.

Serve!

Nutritional Information: 380 calorie; 13.5 g fat (5.2 g saturated fat); 15 mg cholesterol; 235 mg sodium; 65.8 g carbohydrate; 4.2 g dietary fiber; 46.8 g total sugars; 2.5 g protein.

FRESH FRUIT AND CREAM MINI-TARTS

Make every milestone memorable by serving these summery tarts loaded with yummy creamy custard filling. The shortbread tart crust tastes so good even without the filling as it is already loaded with flour, egg yolk, cream, butter, and sweetened with sugar. Top the filling with any fruit of your choice.

Servings: 13-14 tarts

Ingredients

Tart Crust:

1/3 cup **powdered sugar**

1/4 teaspoon **salt**

1 1/2 cups **unbleached flour**

1/2 cup chilled **butter**

1 tablespoon **heavy cream**

1 **egg yolk**

Cream Filling:

2/3 cup **sugar**

2 3/4 cups **milk**

1/8 teaspoon **salt**

1 teaspoon **vanilla extract**

1/4 cup **cornstarch**

2 tablespoons **butter**

4 **egg yolks**

1/4 cup **currant jelly**

Directions

Mix together the sugar, flour and salt in your food processor.

Cut the butter into eight slices and add to the processor. Pulse a few times until the mixture looks like oatmeal.

Combine the egg yolk and cream in a bowl and add to the mixture; pulse to moisten all ingredients. Process for a few seconds until the dough is easy to handle.

Press the dough into a roll, like cookie dough and wrap in plastic. Refrigerate for thirty minutes.

Coat the molds with Baker's Secret, but if using silicone molds, don't use Baker's Secret.

Slice the dough roll into twelve pieces. Roll the dough with a rolling pin between 2 pieces of plastic wrap to form into a circle a bit larger than the tart molds.

Using your fingers, press the dough into the mold and cut off extra dough. Freeze for thirty minutes to overnight.

When ready to use, place the frozen tart shells on a large baking sheet.

Press a small square of aluminum foil into individual crust. Bake for ten minutes at 400 degrees F.

Remove the foil and bake one more time for 3 to 4 minutes until golden brown.

Cream Filling:

Place in a blender the 2 ¾ cups milk, 2/3 cups sugar, ¼ cup cornstarch, 1/8 teaspoon salt and 4 egg yolks.

Process for five seconds and pour the mixture into a two-quart glass microwave safe bowl. Microwave for six minutes on high; whisk after three minutes and later every minute.

Stir in vanilla and butter; whisk until smooth.

Spoon cream filling into the baked tart shell and top with your favorite fruit.

Melt about ¼ cup of currant jelly. Brush the fruits with melted jelly.

Serve!

Nutritional Information: 243 calorie; 12.2 g fat (7.1 g saturated fat); 110 mg cholesterol; 112 mg sodium; 29.7 g carbohydrate; 0.5 g dietary fiber; 15.9 g total sugars; 4.4 g protein.

STRAWBERRY CREAM CHEESE TART

This fruit tart is what you want to enliven your dinner table when celebrating special occasions in your home. The strawberry topping is arranged in concentric pattern to complement with the cream cheese filling and the chocolate ganache. The buttery-soft crust is baked to perfection.

Servings: 8 slices

Ingredients

For the crust:

1 tablespoon **heavy cream**

1 large **egg yolk**

1 ¼ cups **all-purpose flour**

2/3 cup **confectioners' sugar**

1/4 teaspoon **salt**

1/2 teaspoon of **vanilla extracts**

8 tablespoons chilled **unsalted butter** (cut into ½-inch cubes)

For the ganache:

¼ cup **heavy cream**

2 ounces finely chopped **bittersweet chocolate**

1 tablespoon room temperature **unsalted butter**

For the filling:

½ cup **sifted confectioners' sugar**

8 ounces softened **cream cheese**

2 tablespoons **milk** or **heavy cream**

½ teaspoon **vanilla extract**

For topping:

12 ounces fresh sliced **strawberries**

Melted **bittersweet** or **semisweet chocolate** (optional)

Directions

Make the tart shell:

Whisk in a small bowl the cream, vanilla and egg yolk, set aside.

Put together in a food processor the flour, salt and sugar and process until combined.

Spread the pieces of butter on top of the flour mixture and process 15 times for 1-second pulses to cut the butter until it looks like coarse meal.

While the processor is running, gently add the egg mixture and pulse until smooth for twelve seconds.

Place the dough on a sheet of plastic wrap. Press into a six-inch disc. Cover with plastic wrap and chill for 1 hour or up to 2 days.

When the chilled dough is ready to use, allow it to stand at room temperature, unwrap and then roll on a floured counter into a 13" round.

When finished, place it into a 9" tart pan and mold up to the sides, removing excess dough on top. Transfer the tart pan to a large plate. Freeze for half an hour.

Reposition the oven rack in the middle and preheat the oven at 375° F.

Place the tart pan lined with dough on a large baking sheet.

Press a 12" square of aluminum foil into the shell up to the edge and put pie weights on top. Bake for half an hour, rotate halfway through.

Remove the tart pan from the oven and also remove the foil and pie weights. Bake again for five to eight minutes until dark golden brown.

Let cool on wire rack.

Prepare the ganache:

Put the chocolate in a microwave-safe bowl.

Pour the cream in a small saucepan; simmer and pour into the chocolate. Let sit for 1 to 2 minutes until the chocolate has melted. Whisk until it turns into a smooth ganache.

Microwave for ten second intervals if there are bits of chocolate, and whisk in between until totally smooth. Add the butter and whisk.

Evenly spread the ganache on the bottom of the tart shell and let it stand until set.

Make the cream cheese filling:

Beat in a bowl the confectioner's sugar and cream cheese on medium high speed of your blender. Add the milk and vanilla; beat to blend well.

Evenly spread the mixture on top of the cooled chocolate ganache of the baked tart shell.

Arrange the strawberries on top working inward and in concentric circles, and slightly overlapping.

Slowly press the strawberries into the mixture to put them in place.

Mist with optional melted chocolate and chill.

Serve!

Nutritional Information: 417 calorie; 30.7 g fat (19.3 g saturated fat); 109 mg cholesterol; 260 mg sodium; 30.1 g carbohydrate; 1.8 g dietary fiber; 12.3 g total sugars; 6.3 g protein.

EASY MINI PECAN TARTS

This is the easiest and simplest tart ever made that will make you wow because of its sweet taste and nutty texture. You don't have to prepare the crust as you will only need store-bought mini phyllo shells. Each shell is filled with pecan mixture sweetened with honey and brown sugar.

Servings: 15

Ingredients

15 **mini phyllo shells**

1 large **egg**

1 tablespoon **melted butter**

1 tablespoon **honey** or **agave nectar**

2 tablespoons **brown** or **white sugar**

Pinch of **cinnamon**

1/2 teaspoon **vanilla**

1/2 cup **chopped pecans**

Directions

Preheat the oven at 350°F.

Whisk together in a medium-sized mixing bowl, all ingredients excluding the pecans and phyllo shells. Mix until well blended.

Stir in chopped pecans until incorporated.

Place the mini shells on a large baking sheet and fill with a heaping teaspoonful of the pecan mixture.

Bake for ten to fifteen minutes. Let cool completely.

Enjoy!

Nutritional Information: 88 calorie; 4.3 g fat (1.2 g saturated fat); 14 mg cholesterol; 46 mg sodium; 10.5 g carbohydrate; 0.1 g dietary fiber; 2.4 g total sugars; 1.5 g protein.

CUSTARD TARTS

Sweet tooth will be delighted with these fantastic tarts that are filled with flavorful custard sweetened with caster sugar and flavored with vanilla bean. The custard complements well with the soft and buttery crust. The nutmeg is spread on top of custard after removing the tart from oven.

Servings: 6

Ingredients

Pastry:

2 tablespoons **brown sugar**

3 ½ ounces chilled **unsalted butter**, cut into cubes

1 ¼ cups **plain flour**

1 **egg yolk**

1 tablespoon **ice cold water**

Custard:

1 cup of **cream**

1 **vanilla bean** (split and seeds scraped)

2 tablespoons **caster sugar**

3 **egg yolks**

Nutmeg

Directions

Make the pastry:

Put the butter, sugar and flour in a bowl of your food processor. Pulse until the texture bears a resemblance of fine breadcrumbs.

Stir in egg yolk and pulse again to combine.

While the processor is running, drizzle the mixture in cold water and pulse until easy to handle.

Cover the pastry with a sheet of plastic wrap. Chill for one hour.

On a lightly floured counter, roll out the dough into 3 mm thick. Line six ten-centimeter loose bottomed tart tins with dough and trim excess. Chill for 1 hour.

Preheat the oven at 350 degrees F.

Line the tart pans with foil, fill on top with baking weights or pie weights.

Bake for fifteen minutes. Remove the foil and pie weights.

Bake for five minutes more until golden, let cool.

Bring the cream in a saucepan to a boil; remove from heat. Stir in vanilla bean and seeds and leave it there for 1 hour or overnight to infuse the flavor.

Heat the oven to 250 degrees F.

Discard the vanilla pod. Stir in sugar and egg yolks, whisking to combine. Strain through a fine mesh sieve directly into a bowl and pour into the tart base.

Bake for twenty minutes until cooked.

Spread on top with chopped nutmeg. Let cool.

Serve!

Nutritional Information: 335 calorie; 21 g fat (12.1 g saturated fat); 183 mg cholesterol; 115 mg sodium; 31.4 g carbohydrate; 1.8 g dietary fiber; 9.9 g total sugars; 5.5 g protein.

PUMPKIN PIE MINI TARTS

What makes these tarts unique, is they are handy and you can take this anywhere in your Bento box because of their small sizes. The mini tarts are filled with spicy filling consisting of cinnamon, ginger, cloves and allspice with pumpkin, cream and milk for a creamier texture.

Servings: 15 mini-tarts

Ingredients

Tart Crust:

1/3 cup **powdered sugar**

1/4 teaspoon **salt**

1 1/2 cups **unbleached flour**

1/2 cup chilled **butter**

1 tablespoon **heavy cream**

1 **egg yolk**

For the filling:

1 teaspoon **cinnamon**

3/4 cup **brown sugar**

1/2 teaspoon **ginger**

2 **eggs** plus 1 **egg yolk**

1/8 teaspoon **cloves**

1/8 teaspoon **allspice**

1/2 teaspoon **salt**

1 (15 ounces) can **pure pumpkin**

3/4 cup **milk**

1/2 cup **heavy cream**

Directions

Prepare the Crust:

Combine in a food processor the flour, salt and sugar.

Cut the butter into eight slices and add to the processor. Pulse a few times until the texture looks like oatmeal.

Combine the egg yolk and cream in a bowl and add to the processor. Pulse until the mixture is moistened.

Let the processor run for a few seconds until the dough comes together and press into a roll similar to refrigerated cookie dough.

Wrap the dough in plastic and refrigerate for thirty minutes.

Coat the molds with generous amount of Baker's Secret if not using silicone molds.

Slice the dough roll into fifteen to sixteen pieces and flatten between two sheets of plastic wrap to form into a circle slightly bigger than the molds.

With your fingers, press the circle into the tart mold and trim off excess dough. Freeze for thirty minutes longer.

When ready to use, place the tart shells on a cookie sheet. Press a small foil down into the crust up to the sides.

Bake for ten minutes at 400 degrees F.

Prepare the pie filling:

Combine in a medium-sized bowl the brown sugar, cinnamon, cloves, ginger, salt and allspice.

Whisk the pumpkin puree and eggs together in a separate bowl.

Pour the spice mixture into the pumpkin mixture and whisk until combined.

Pour the milk and cream; whisk until smooth.

Fill the prebaked tart with filling and bake for fifteen to twenty minutes at 350 degrees F. Let cool on a rack.

Chill for 30 minutes longer before serving.

Serve!

Nutritional Information: 203 calorie; 10.8 g fat (6.6 g saturated fat); 79 mg cholesterol; 182 mg sodium; 23.2 g carbohydrate; 1.5 g dietary fiber; 11.5 g total sugars; 3.3 g protein.

No-Bake Salted Dark Chocolate Mascarpone Tart

This weekend, treat your family with this no-bake rich chocolate tart made with Oreo cookie crust and filled with whipped cream mascarpone filling and topped with creamy chocolate ganache sprinkled with sea salt flakes. It will be ready in 25 minutes.

Servings: 8-10

Ingredients

6 tablespoons melted **unsalted butter**

2 cups **Oreo cookie crumbs**

1/2 cup cold **whipping cream**

1 teaspoon **vanilla**

3/4 cup **sugar**

275 grams softened **mascarpone cheese**

8 ounces **dark chocolate chips** or **semi-sweet chocolate**

1 cup **whipping cream**

1 to 2 teaspoons **sea salt flakes**

Directions

Combine in a bowl the melted butter and Oreo cookie crumbs. Press the crumbs on the bottom and up to the sides of a 9-inch tart pan. Freeze for 30 minutes or more.

With a hand mixer, whip the whipping cream until soft peaks are formed. Set aside.

Whip in another bowl the sugar, mascarpone and vanilla until combined. Stir in whipped cream; blend until smooth.

Pour the filling into the cold Oreo crust and return to the freezer to set for 1 hour.

While waiting for the crust to firm up, prepare the ganache.

Pour the whipping cream into a small saucepan on medium heat. Stir often and simmer.

Pour the whipping cream over the chocolate chips, whisking until smooth. Let cool and pour into the frozen tart.

Chill for two hours until ready to serve.

Enjoy!

Nutritional Information: 463 calorie; 36.6 g fat (87.2 g cholesterol); 346.1 mg sodium; 31.1 g carbohydrate; 26.3 g total sugars; 4 g protein.

Snickers Blondie Tart

This tart mimics the Snickers by making it appear like one. You will love its gooey milk chocolate ganache poured all over the salted caramel. The roasted unsalted peanuts lurk underneath the caramel. The tart base is a mixture of peanut butter, cream, egg, flour, brown sugar and baking powder.

Servings: 10

Ingredients

1/2 cup **peanut butter**

4 tablespoons softened **unsalted butter**

3/4 cup loosely packed **light brown sugar**

1 large **egg**

1/2 teaspoon **baking powder**

3/4 cup **all-purpose flour**

1/2 cup **dry roasted unsalted peanuts**

1/4 teaspoon **kosher salt**

1/4 cup **heavy cream**

4 ounces **salted caramel sauce**

2 ounces chopped **milk chocolate**

Directions

Preheat the oven at 350 degrees Fahrenheit.

Place the brown sugar, peanut butter and butter in a blender and cream on medium speed until soft and fluffy. Stir in egg and mix thoroughly until incorporated.

Add the flour, salt and baking powder and mix until fully blended.

Spread on the bottom and up to the sides of your rectangular tart pan.

Bake for twenty minutes until the edges are golden and the center is set. Let cool.

Evenly spread the peanuts on the bottom of the tart and drizzle the top with salted caramel.

Heat the heavy cream until the edges show small bubbles and pour all over the chopped chocolate. Stir to combine, slightly cool and pour evenly over the tart.

Let ganache set for several minutes. Slice.

Serve!

Nutritional Information: 343 calorie; 19 g fat (7 g saturated fat); 40 mg cholesterol; 128 mg sodium; 38g carbohydrate; 2 g dietary fiber; 21 g total sugars; 7 g protein.

CHOCOLATE & PEANUT BUTTER MOUSSE TARTS

The extra delicious taste of these tarts is always unforgettable, thanks to the buttery Oreo crust topped with a creamy chocolate layer and a layer of peanut butter mousse. The remaining chocolate mixture is spread on top of the mousse and ends with peanut butter chips

Servings: 4 4-inch tarts

Ingredients

Crust:

3 tablespoons melted **unsalted butter**

15 **Oreo cookies**

Chocolate layer:

1/2 cup **heavy cream**

6 ounces chopped **milk chocolate**

1 teaspoon **vanilla extract**

1 tablespoon **light corn syrup**

Peanut Butter Mousse:

1/2 cup **powdered sugar**

1 3/4 cups **heavy cream**, divided

1 cup **peanut butter**

Topping:

Peanut butter chips

Directions

For the crust:

Preheat the oven at 350°Fahrenheit.

128

Prepare four pieces of 4" tart pans and lightly coat with nonstick cooking spray.

Set the tart pans on a rimmed baking sheet.

Process the Oreo cookies in your food processor until pulverized. Add in the melted butter; process until moistened.

Equally distribute the mixture into the prepared tart pans and press into the bottom and up to the sides. Bake for five minutes until set. Let crust cool completely.

For the chocolate layer:

In a large glass measuring cup, combine the chocolate, vanilla, corn syrup and cream.

Microwave the mixture for 1 ½ minutes, and stir until the chocolate has melted and creamy and the entire mixture turns dark and smooth.

Refrigerate one-fourth of the mixture and divide the rest between the crusts. Level the mixture up to the bottom and freeze until set.

For the peanut butter mousse:

Place ¾ cup of the heavy cream in a heatproof bowl and microwave in twenty-second bursts; stir after each burst until melted.

Add the vanilla and let cool at room temperature.

Beat in a bowl of a hand mixer with whisk attachment the powdered sugar and remaining one cup heavy cream on high speed until the mixture thickens but no peaks are formed.

Gently fold the mixture into the cooled peanut butter mixture.

When there are no streaks left, spoon the peanut butter mouse into the cold chocolate layer. Refrigerate for one hour.

When the tarts have firmed up, remove from fridge as well as the remaining chocolate mixture.

Stir the chocolate mixture to loosen and place in a Ziploc bag. Snip off one corner and drizzle on top of tarts.

Spread the peanut butter chips on top. Chill for up to two days until ready to serve.

Enjoy!

Nutritional Information: 1218 calorie; 87.2 g fat (40.4 g saturated fat); 117 mg cholesterol; 564 sodium; 93.2 g carbohydrate; 7.1 g dietary fiber; 65.3 g total sugars; 25.6 g protein.

BRIE AND BLACKBERRY TARTLETS

These tartlets will prove that they are not complicated to prepare. It calls for 4 ingredients only and you need a ready-made pie crust to make the tart in a jiffy. A small chunk of brie is placed on top of the refrigerated pie crust before baking. A spoonful of blackberry jam and a fresh blackberry are placed on top of tart.

Servings: 24

Ingredients

Blackberries

Blackberry jam

1 package refrigerated **pie crust**

1 (8 ounces) package of **brie**, rind removed

Directions

Preheat the oven at 400 degrees F.

Coat your mini muffin tin with nonstick cooking spray.

Press a small portion of the crust into the bottom and up to the sides of the prepared muffin tin.

Place on top of tin, a small brie chunk. Bake for ten minutes. Let the tart cool in the oven and remove from pan. Let cool.

Top the cooled tart with a spoonful of blackberry jam and top with one fresh blackberry.

Serve!

Nutritional Information: 686 calorie; 44.1 g fat (7.8 g saturated fat); 9 mg cholesterol; 877 mg sodium; 64.1 g carbohydrate; 1.8 g dietary fiber; 6.3 g total sugars; 7.6 g protein.

Salted Caramel & Chocolate Truffle Tart

This luscious tart is remarkably a total package with its creamy and crunchy shortbread crust. But it does not end there as the salted caramel is added to the crust and a layer of chocolate ganache is next in line with finishing touches of truffles and sprinkled with cocoa powder.

Servings: 1 tart (about 10-12 servings)

Ingredients

Crust:

1/2 teaspoon **vanilla extract**

1 tablespoon **heavy cream**

1 **egg yolk**

1/4 teaspoon **salt**

2/3 cup **powdered sugar**

1 1/4 cups **flour**

8 tablespoons (1 stick) chilled **unsalted butter**, cut into 1/4" pieces

Caramel:

25 **wrapped Kraft** or **Brachs caramels**

1/2 teaspoon **good quality sea salt**

2 tablespoons **heavy cream**

Ganache:

1/2 cup **heavy cream**

4 ounces **semi-sweet chocolate**

Handful of **unsweetened cocoa powder**

15 **Lindt LINDOR truffles** cut into half

Directions

Prepare the crust:

132

Whisk in a small bowl the cream, vanilla and egg yolk, set aside.

Blend in a food processor the flour, salt and sugar for five seconds. Add in the butter cubes; pulse for fifteen seconds until it has a strong resemblance with cornmeal.

Add the egg while the gadget is running; process for 12 seconds until it forms into dough. Cover with plastic wrap; refrigerate for 15 minutes.

Roll in the middle of two sheets of plastic wrap into ¼-inch thick with the size of a 14x4-inch rectangle tart pan or a round pan.

Remove and discard the top sheet of plastic wrap, flipping the dough over into the pan with overhang.

With your hand, ease the dough into the bottom of the pan by lifting the edge and press into the corners with your other hand. Leave overhang as is.

Press the dough into the grove-sides of the pan. If possible add dough bits to patch up any thin parts. Roll the rolling pin on top of the pan to remove excess dough. Cover with plastic wrap and freeze for thirty minutes.

Preheat the oven at 375 degrees F.

Remove the tart from freezer and discard the plastic wrap.

Slowly press a sheet of foil into the tart shell up to the edges. Place pie weights or dry beans on top of foil and place the tart on a baking sheet. Bake for thirty minutes.
Slowly remove the dry beans or pie weights after thirty minutes, then discard the foil and bake for five to ten minutes until golden brown. Let cool.

Prepare the caramel:

Remove the wrappers of caramels and put in a heatproof bowl with the heavy cream.

Microwave the mixture at 50 percent power for three to five minutes, taking a closer look from time to time.

When the caramels have melted, stir vigorously and stir in salt. Let cool for a few minutes and pour into the cooled crust. Chill for ten minutes until firmed up.

Cut the truffles into halves, set aside.

Prepare the ganache:

Chop the semi-sweet chocolate into small bits. In a microwave safe bowl, heat the cream in the microwave until warmed through.

Add in the chopped chocolate, let sit for a minute. Stir afterwards until the chocolate has totally melted and incorporated.

Freeze and stir every ten minutes to reach its desired texture.

Pour over caramel layer and evenly spread with an offset spatula.

Arrange the truffles on top of ganache in an even layer. Sprinkle on top with cocoa powder. Refrigerate for 15 minutes.

Serve!

Nutritional Information: 1064 calorie; 55 g fat (34.2 g saturated fat); 67 mg cholesterol; 280 mg sodium; 138.9 g carbohydrate; 4.8 g dietary fiber; 87.7 g total sugars; 10.7 g protein.

PEACHES & CREAM TART

This fruit tart offers excitement to your dinner. A crust made of almonds, butter and coconut macaroon cookies are topped with the cream cheese filling and another layer of peaches and raspberries perched on top of filling. The fruits are glazed with honey and apricot preserve mixture.

Servings: 10

Ingredients

For the Crust:

3 tablespoons melted **butter**

1 cup **ground almonds**

2 cups crumbled soft **coconut macaroon cookies**

For the Filling:

8 ounces softened **cream cheese**

1/2 cup **heavy whipping cream**

2 teaspoons **orange juice**

1/3 cup **sugar**

1/4 teaspoon of **almond extract**

1 teaspoon of **vanilla extract**

1/2 cup **fresh raspberries**

4 medium peeled and sliced **peaches**

2 teaspoons **honey**

1/4 cup **apricot preserves**

Directions

For the Crust:

Preheat the oven at 350 degrees F.

Crumble the coconut macaroon cookies in a food processor in two batches. Pour into a large bowl. Place the almonds in the food processor and process.

Return the cookie crumbs in the food processor together with the almonds. Stir in melted butter and process until incorporated.

Press the cookie crumbs on the bottom and up to the sides of an 11″ fluted tart pan with detachable bottom.

Set the pan on your baking sheet; bake for 12 to 14 minutes until golden brown. Let cool fully on a wire rack.

For the Filling:

Beat with a hand mixer the whipping cream until fluffy and soft. Set aside.

Beat in another bowl the cream cheese and sugar until the texture is smooth.

Add the orange juice, almond and vanilla extracts and beat. Fold the cream cheese mixture into whipped cream.

Evenly layer the cream cheese filling over the cookie crust.

Neatly arrange the raspberries and peaches on top of filling.

Combine in a small saucepan the honey and apricot preserves; cook and stir on low until melted.

Brush the glaze on top of fruit. Chill.

Serve!

Nutritional Information: 444 calorie; 24.3 g fat (14 g saturated fat); 42 mg cholesterol; 209 mg sodium; 54.9 g carbohydrate; 3.4 g dietary fiber; 49.7 g total sugars; 6.2 g protein.

MANGO TART WITH VANILLA BEAN PASTRY CREAM

Experience the tropics with this mango tart paired with vanilla bean pastry cream. The buttery crust is topped with a creamy filling made with the perfect blend of egg yolks, flour, milk, cornstarch, and sugar and flavored with vanilla bean. The topmost part is filled with rosette patterned mango slices.

Servings: 12

Ingredients

For the crust:

1/3 cup **confectioners' sugar**

1 cup **all-purpose flour**

1/2 cup (1 stick) cold and cubed **unsalted butter**

1/8 teaspoon **salt**

For the filling:

1/4 cup **sugar**

3 large **egg yolks**

2 tablespoons **cornstarch**

2 tablespoons **all-purpose flour**

1/2 vanilla **bean**, split into lengthwise

1 1/4 cups **whole milk**

3 large **mangoes** cut into thin slices

Directions

Make the crust:

Put the flour, salt and sugar in a bowl of your food processor with a pastry blade attachment.

Pulse the mixture and add the cubed butter; pulse until the ingredients are fully incorporated and the texture is akin to large clumps.

Coat a 9" detachable-bottomed nonstick tart pan with cooking spray.

Place the dough into the pan and press evenly to mold the base and sides of the crust. Prick the bottom of crust with fork.

Cover the entire pan with plastic wrap. Freeze for fifteen minutes.

Preheat the oven at 425 degrees F.

Discard the plastic wrap and transfer the tart pan on a baking sheet. Bake for thirteen to fifteen minutes until golden brown. Remove tart pan from oven and let tart cool in the pan.

Push the bottom of the tart pan if puffed up and place on a serving dish.

Make the filling:

Whisk in a medium bowl the sugar and egg yolks. Sift the cornstarch and flour into the bowl, whisking until the mixture is smooth. Pour the milk into a medium saucepan.

Prepare the vanilla bean by scraping into the milk.

Add the vanilla bean to the saucepan and let boil until the milk starts to produce a foamy texture. Remove immediately from heat and discard the vanilla bean.

Gently whisk the milk directly into the mixture. Whisk to avoid curdling and pour into a saucepan on medium heat.

Cook and whisk often, until boiling. Whisk for thirty to sixty seconds until the mixture is consistent.

Pour the hot mixture into a bowl, cover with plastic wrap to let it touch the pastry cream.

Position the bowl in a much bigger bowl with ice water to let it cool.

Start whisking the mixture when it is already at room temperature to remove lumps.

When everything is smooth, pour the pastry cream into the tart shell.

Neatly arrange the mango slices on top of pastry cream working in the center going towards outside, to form into flower petals.

Chill for two hours in the refrigerator or place in the freezer with cover for up to 2 days. Slice.

Enjoy!

Nutritional Information: 220 calorie; 10.5 g fat (6.1 g saturated fat); 75 mg cholesterol; 91 mg sodium; 29.6 g carbohydrate; 1.9 g dietary fiber; 18.3 g total sugars; 3.6 g protein.

CONCLUSION

Thank you so much for downloading this Book. We at Savour Press hope this book has increased your knowledge regarding some mouthwatering tart recipes. This Book contains a curated list of what we believe to be the 45 most delicious dessert tarts which cover a variety of cooking methods, flavors and tastes. All different categories of tarts are represented such as your mousse tart, cream tart, mini tarts, tartlets, chocolate tarts, crumble tarts and many more.

During our sabbatical leave, we reached a consensus that all recipes should not be as complicated as you think, as we all know that tarts are a bit complex when it comes to its preparation. The ingredients should be available in both online and offline stores and they are easy on your pocket. Whenever you are requested to prepare a dessert, at least you have something delicious to offer. We hope you will enjoy cooking with these recipes.

Thanks again for your support.

Happy Cooking!

Made in the USA
Middletown, DE
12 April 2019